SIX DAYS AT RONNIE SCOTT'S:

Billy Cobham on Jazz Fusion and the Act of Creation

BRIAN K. GRUBER

Copyright © 2018 Brian K. Gruber and Creative Multimedia Concepts, Inc.

www.grubermedia.com

All rights reserved under the Berne Convention. No part of this publication may be reproduced, distributed, or transmitted in any form or by any means, including photocopying, recording, or other electronic or mechanical methods, without the prior written permission of the publisher, except in the case of brief quotations embodied in critical reviews and certain other noncommercial uses permitted by copyright law. For permission requests, write to the publisher, at the email address below.

briankgruber@gmail.com

ISBN-10: 1717493009
ISBN-13: 978-1717493002

CONTENTS

Acknowledgments v
Preface vii
1 In The Beginning 1
2 Kids 31
3 Miles, Mahavishnu, Montreux 67
4 Ronnie Scott, 52nd Street And The Left Behind Snare Drum 103
5 The Art Of The Rhythm Section 129
6 And On The Sixth Day 161
   About The Author 187
   Billy Cobham Discography 189

Each chapter has a Spotify playlist (Billy Cobham One, Billy Cobham Two, etc.) including relevant tunes, artists, and genres. Enjoy each chapter's soundtrack.

ACKNOWLEDGMENTS

There are a small number of music venues worldwide that offer a legacy and experience akin to that of a cathedral; a sacred space, with rich history, the highest standards, and the promise of a transformative experience. Ronnie Scott's, certainly the gold standard of UK jazz clubs, quite possibly the most iconic in all of Europe, welcomed me with full access and no small measure of hospitality. Several of the club's principals including co-owner Michael Watt and resident "jazzhead" and booker Paul Pace offered critical insights, while master impresario Simon Cooke enabled my smooth and efficient work time there. It was a memorable experience and I am grateful to the club's staff and management.

Bill introduced me to the band members at the first rehearsal and there would be no book without their gracious acceptance; many are interviewed in these pages. More than that, they allowed me to witness the alchemy of creation up close. It was a master class and some of those horn riffs are indelibly imprinted in my brain. As to Guy Barker, his masterful storytelling and kindness are a persistent theme of the book.

Faina Cobham dashes about before, during and after each show with whirlwind speed and makes sure the trains run on time. Thank you, Fai, for enduring my constant requests and prima donna requirements.

When I was unsure how to form the project, my friend Mark Phinney provided the final push forward on Koh Phangan, validating the idea and flying to London to provide the unique perspective of a superfan.

Iain Donnelly, fresh from the launch of his Saraswati Publishing venture in Cambodia, edited the book, tirelessly providing literary and musical guidance and forcing a focus on the reader's point of view. Paul Price, Bill's CD designer, brought his unique creative gifts to bringing the cover to life. The cover photograph is the work of photographer Ken Hunt, Whole Earth Images, who has generously allowed for its use.

Thanks to the parents, teachers and students of Soho Parish Primary School for sharing their big day, with a special tip of the hat to Pete Letanka.

I am thankful to friends and family, some involved in the *ShowGoTV* jazz streaming project, who nurtured and supported my interest in Bill's work, in jazz, and in music. Don and Stephen Shapiro, my deceased brother Jeff, Bill O'Luanaigh, Lou Borrelli and Bob Ellis, Kristi Vandenbosch, Tony Berman, Nancy Balik, Erik Herz, Hardy Hemmingway, Katherine Ajk, among many others. Sebastian Wagner came to one of the shows and sparked the idea of creating a Spotify soundtrack for each chapter (check out the playlists, *Billy Cobham One*, *Billy Cobham Two*, etc.). Bill and I would never have met without Marynell Maloney's grace, charm, and spectacular Chenailles chateau setting.

Bill Bruford warned that I would be "spending many hours indoors" transcribing and organizing the tens of hours of interviews for the book. Big thanks to the interviewees who gave freely of their time without hesitation. Conversations with band members, club executives, fans, reviewers, and crew took place during the week at Ronnie Scott's as indicated in these pages. Some conversations were conducted just prior to or shortly after the shows.

The book is an oral history and I had a rich education studying the style and works of masters of the genre such as Studs Terkel. I cut my interviewing teeth years ago at C-SPAN, at *FORA.tv* and *ShowGoTV*, and during the writing of *WAR: The Afterparty*. Sharing the stories of great men and women in their own words is a grand privilege.

This book is a labor of love and a tribute to one of the world's great musical storytellers, Billy Cobham. I'll let the book speak to my thoughts of his work and his life. I am grateful for the many hours he devoted to this project and for the opportunity to learn from a master and a friend.

Thanks to all those involved in the project. I had a ball.

PREFACE

There was a domestic war in the United States, a growing 'generation gap' in the late '60s and early '70s even as the conflict in Vietnam was escalating. I was 14 in March of 1970, my brother Jeff a wise but wild role model at the advanced age of 19.

My earliest memory is of my mother Claire tying my shoes at three years old at our Legion Street, Brooklyn tenement. But my fiercest early memory was Mom raging at Jeff in our East New York, Brooklyn housing-project apartment upon finding anti-war paraphernalia. Five decades later, I can tell you exactly what one button said: "The Great Society, *Bombs, Bullets, Bullshit.*"

It was a political and cultural divide and music was smack on the front lines. Jazz, firmly established as America's popular music, had been overwhelmed by rock and roll, which my parents despised. Anti-war buttons aside, and well before music might be safely sequestered in iTunes libraries, vinyl 'records' littered teenage bedroom floors, with designs, liner notes, and musical forms aspiring to subvert the existing order. Relatively clueless, as I trailed my brother's political and musical evolution by a half decade, I could tell the degree of subversion by the pitch of my mother's voice.

"*The Sad Sad World of Mothers and Fathers??!?*" That *Brute Force* title was not well received by Claire, nor were Frank Zappa lyrics, or odd, loud explosions of sound taunting my parents' more civilized record collection, tucked neatly in the hi-fi stereo cabinet.

Billy Eckstine was a favorite of Mom's. As was Frank Sinatra. There was Cab Calloway, who my father hired in the '30s to perform at his Brooklyn house party. And lots of Al Jolson, who Dad could imitate flawlessly. Some of the records did find some purchase amongst the kids. Dave Brubeck's odd-metered *Take Five*. And the first jazz album that turned my head, the breakthrough bossa nova classic, *Getz/Gilberto*.

In March 1970, President Richard Nixon was promising peace with honor in Vietnam while striking out at the Paris peace talks. But my dad Sol and brother Jeff found their own way to harmonize personal and musical differences; they took me to my first concert. The Fillmore East was Bill Graham's Manhattan rock and roll mecca, and a unique breeding ground for visual and musical experimentation. The headliner, Neil Young and Crazy Horse, was preceded by the Steve Miller Blues Band. With Miles Davis opening, and performing, among other things, the breakthrough release that is widely considered the birth of jazz-rock 'fusion,' *Bitches Brew*.

No, that's not quite right. Davis played second.

> *I was opening for this sorry-ass cat named Steve Miller...didn't have shit going for him, so I'm pissed because I got to open for this non-playing motherfucker just because he had one or two sorry-ass records out. So, I would come late and he would have to go on first, and then when we go there, we just smoked the motherfucking place and everybody dug it, including Bill.* [1]

A few weeks before, William Emmanuel Cobham Junior found himself in a studio recording tracks for *Bitches Brew*, along with John McLaughlin and an astounding cast of artists who would go on to transform jazz and popular music.

I first met Billy Cobham just before my birthday in August of 2010. I was spending a good part of the summer at friend Marynell Maloney's home in France's Loire River valley. A few days earlier, just across the river in Jargeau, Joan of Arc's old stomping grounds, I was reading in an open-air plaza, sipping a glass of local wine, when three musicians suddenly set up a few yards away. They proceeded to perform an acoustic rendition of Chick Corea's *Spain*. After their shockingly good performance, I introduced myself and got their card. Marynell invited them to perform at the birthday party and I casually suggested Bill might join them. She rightly scorned the idea, a legend playing with local musicians, won't happen. But after dinner, as they played on the patio under a starry sky, he did just that on a tiny drum set. A friend of Bill's remarked, "He can't help himself."

In the years since, I have seen Bill perform in Paris, Milan, Rio, and numerous U.S. cities. As he plugged his iPad into my car audio system, he would share a never-ending stream of stories that were not only insightful,

---

[1] Davis, Miles with Troupe, Quincy. 1989. *Miles: The Autobiography*. Touchstone/Simon & Schuster. p. 301.

bawdy, and astounding, but also provided a unique panorama of the last half-century of American music. So, when Bill told me he was collaborating with Britain's hottest arranger, jazz trumpeter Guy Barker, to orchestrate and perform his oeuvre with a 17-piece big band at Europe's premiere jazz club Ronnie Scott's, I thought; why not hang out backstage, in rehearsals and at the bar during the six-day run and finally gather those stories. Not a biography, but an oral history exploring six decades of music, an improvised series of encounters during one special week. Talk to the greats who have played with him, club owners, music critics, friends, and family, to explore the source of Billy Cobham's musical power and joy, this jazz fusion pioneer and innovator, and discover what motivates him to continue to create at the age of 73.

Guy is calling the six-day residency at Ronnie's "a celebration of Bill's life and work in music." Billy Cobham, a guy voted year after year as the greatest drummer in the world, considered the greatest living jazz fusion drummer, one-time bandmate of Miles Davis, Randy Brecker, Mahavishnu Orchestra, Jimi Hendrix, Ron Carter, George Duke, Stan Getz, Muhammad Ali (!), George Benson, Freddie Hubbard, Billy Taylor, Horace Silver, from incarnations of the Grateful Dead and Jack Bruce to Peter Gabriel's WOMAD, the list seems endless.

Back in the chateau's expansive dining room, I asked Bill if he had any birthday advice for me. He answered without hesitation, "Live your life with reckless abandon."

I'm working on it.

Brian Gruber
May 18, 2018
Koh Phangan, Thailand

1 IN THE BEGINNING

Brooklyn, New York, Spring 1947

A three-year-old boy alone in his room on a Saturday morning is master of the universe.

The rest of the week is regulated by Ivy and William Senior. What to eat, what to wear, what to hear. Bath time, shopping time, promenade time. And this just months into the cacophony of Bedford-Stuyvesant life. *The Cristobal* transports the family from Panamanian shantytown Colon to Manhattan's west side, then they're on to Harlem, then Brooklyn. *Bed-Stuy*, Chauncey Street, across from Fulton Park, a brownstone clustered with other Caribbean households.

Saturday morning at the park is time for driving percussive beats, untamed power. The boy notices the Puertorriqueño, Cubano, Colombiano, Panameno congueros in the neighborhood, coming off the 'A' train on Utica Avenue all week long. Exhausted bus drivers, filthy construction laborers, put-upon janitors, exasperated store owners, all beholden, *controlled* by someone or something. The twenty-something Nicaraguan accosted by his girlfriend with furious accusations, the older fellow burdened by some damn thing. A week of complaining, protesting, bemoaning. Then…Saturday comes.

It's 1947, so Saturday morning cartoons on black-and-white televisions are a decade away. He'll have to wait till he's eight to make his weekly trek with kids on the block to the local movie theatre for six hours of movies, shorts, cartoons, and trailers. These men, some just back from World War II service in Europe or the Pacific, some feeling sucked dry from a week of bosses, cops, families, life, exude power and joy, their laughs are fierce, fat, and ecstatic. He is captivated, the beats filling his room. Here's an early lesson: joy, power, freedom, human connection flow from the hands of men who can drive a beat forward.

Chauncey Street, Brooklyn, June 7, 2017

I am standing in front of Billy Cobham's childhood home.

After taking photos of the house and neighborhood, I sit for a while on the Fulton Park bench across the narrow street, taking in the families, couples, and schoolkids walking on by. My own birthplace, 90 Legion Street is a half-hour walk away, just past Pitkin Avenue, where my parents would dress up and push my baby carriage past the haberdasheries and delis during Sunday promenades. My plan tonight is 6pm dinner with a high school friend in the city, followed by a walk down one-time jazz mecca 52nd Street, midnight jazz at Small's, then an early morning taxi ride to JFK to catch my flight to London Heathrow.

After emailing photos of Chauncey Street to Bill at his home in Switzerland, I begin my afternoon trek to neighboring Brownsville. These streets were walked, passed, visited hundreds of times by my parents Sol and Claire. The 1920 Census reveals my father's family home is a short two miles away. My daughter Jennie chose to live here in Bed-Stuy while going to grad school at Sarah Lawrence, foregoing the tony comforts of the school's Bronxville location. I notice a response from Bill on my phone and open it to find that I had the address wrong. The house was *89* Chauncey, not 93. I walk double-time to Legion Street only to find that #90 no longer exists. Two older men eye me suspiciously from a stoop. One confronts me. "Hey, your shoes are untied." I circle back to Chauncey Street by taxi to take photos of the correct house, then take the 'A' train to the city, the beginning of my long journey to London.

Our Gang

In the weeks before our London rendezvous, Bill and I talk over Skype about our Brooklyn childhoods and how our early perceptions of life, music, family, and prosperity were formed.

BILLY COBHAM: There were no fridges till three or four years later. The iceman would ring the bell, chisel a block to fit the refrigerator. Came around in wooden trucks. The ice was covered in a wet cloth, packed in mounds, very heavy frozen blocks. The knife and scissors-sharpening guy, a lot of hawkers came to the door at that time.

BRIAN GRUBER: It sounds like you enjoyed growing up in Brooklyn.

COBHAM: Sure. It didn't last long enough. The Dodgers left in '57, along with the Giants. We moved around '57/'58 to Queens. My uncle Winston bought a house in South Jamaica and by that time my grandmother had come to live with us from Panama. We lived with my uncle's family for a while, before they moved further east to Long Island.

Back in Bed-Stuy, I was part of a small group of kids that used to hang around together. Didn't see each other that much in the winters. We were all from Caribbean families, not really happy about being in the cold. We would hang out a lot in the summer. It was my version of *Our Gang*. We would go to the Apollo Theater, on Fulton and Nostrand. At 10 o'clock in the morning, we opened the place up. What was so hip about being there in the summer was that we would come with lunch pails, with sandwiches and a thermos with a cold drink. Our folks knew exactly where we were from 10am to about three or four in the afternoon. All they showed at that time was cartoons, then *Captain Marvel*, Buster Crabbe as *Flash Gordon*, *Hopalong Cassidy*, *Lash LaRue*, Gene Autry, Roy Rogers and Dale Evans, *The Shadow*, the *Green Lantern*. We would sit there, a small group of about 10 of us from Chauncey Street, part of a huge group of kids throughout, just roaring, rocking it. That theater made money on us. For 25 cents per kid, they babysat us while Mom was cleaning the house, Dad cleaning the car...

GRUBER: You were saying each block might have a concentration of nationalities, Panamanians on Chauncey Street, Colombians or Cubans on another. Were your friends Panamanians?

COBHAM: Between Lewis and Stuyvesant, it was Barbadians, Trinidadians, but black Panamanians, not 'Castilian' Panamanians, who would still consider themselves racially Spanish and, therefore, superior in social stature. The black community who came up from the Caribbean area could be from Guatemala, Belize, and they would flock together and hang really close. Just one block away, there was a Puerto Rican community and they went to the Catholic Church at Halsey or Reed. We went to the Baptist Church or St. Philips Episcopal Church, north of us. A different community every four or five blocks, same kind of people before it would filter out into another ethnic or religious environment. There was one public school, P.S. 35 on Lewis, four or five blocks up the road. *(Bill rattles off precise walking directions to each place mentioned, with distances, street names and ethnic boundaries.)*

GRUBER: I remember the same experience at the Biltmore Theatre in my East New York, Brooklyn neighborhood. We terrorized the white-uniformed 'matrons,' throwing Jujubes and whatnot when they turned around. There was plenty of crime in Brooklyn but a weird sense of security walking to the theater. By 13, we traveled alone on buses and subways into the city. Were you a good student?

COBHAM: No. I fell into a blank area, a body that went to school because that was required. What we studied? I don't even remember. What I do remember is a map of Africa, where there was an outline of the continent with two eyes and a broad nose with wide nostrils, and red lips. *Africa: The Dark Continent*. It did not identify any names of any countries. Communist countries were China, yellow, with Peking as the only city and the red Soviet Union with a hammer and sickle, Moscow the only city spanning 11 time zones. Those are the books that came to my school. To this day, the conquerors write the history. Why did I come to Europe? With all of that happening, I needed to get answers for myself and draw my own conclusions.

GRUBER: Do you remember living in Panama?

COBHAM: No, but I remember the ship, *The Cristobal*. It was scuttled 10-15 years ago. Brought me and my mom to New York. Dad was already there for a job. We had Panamanian sponsors who had already established themselves in the states. Never went back until 2005.

All around us, where I was brought up, there were small townships, Rainbow City, Silver City. Gatun, which is now a lake. My family was definitely in one of the poorest parts of the world. The gold and silver standard. Panamanians and Americans were paid the same amount for work but white Americans got paid in gold, Panamanians got paid in silver, same number but a fraction of what gold was worth.

GRUBER: Do you have a first memory of music that has stayed with you?

COBHAM: What I can remember is what I heard first. My father was a gifted pianist. He made extra money in a bar, he could make people sound good when they were drunk. Never read a note of music. He was a lexicon of music, loved jazz, loved calypso, loved Latin music, and he loved some classical. Nothing to do with rock and roll or soul, that wasn't his thing. If you were a little tipsy and asked, "Do you know *Sweet Lorraine?*" Dad would say, well, "I don't know," then start accompanying (*Bill starts singing Sweet Lorraine, "I'm as happy as a baby boy..."*) A guy's friends would say, "Hey Joe, we didn't know you could sing!" My dad made more money in six to seven hours at that bar than he made all month as a statistician for Bronx General Hospital. Fascinating to watch. Everyone walked away absolutely happy.

GRUBER: What do you feel when you tell that story?

COBHAM: It's kind of funny. It is at the foundation of how I perform. I am trying to enhance whatever positive elements other musicians bring to the table. That's what my Art of the Rhythm Section school is about - interpreting what your colleague presents you with. "This is how I feel about what you're feeling." The frequencies are in harmony with everything that you do. That is what makes music meaningful.

When it got warmer, in the spring, early Saturday mornings - never on Sunday, being in a Latin American community, everyone goes to church - a lot of the immigrants would come together, Panamanians, Cubans, Puerto Ricans, Nicaraguans and play in a *conjunto*, a group of drummers, 10 or 15 guys. In Robert Fulton Park, on steps on the Stuyvesant Avenue side, like a gazebo, big brick, cinder block wall, and the sound would reverberate through it. Timbales, conga, tumbao, bongos, quinto. They were paying tribute to home, reaching out through the drums, communicating with whomever they could. I don't know if it was *Candomble* or black magic, but it was very dynamic. I would wake up to that. Then the folks would get up and turn on the old Crosley radio, big huge thing that stood in the corner, incredibly full sound.

GRUBER: How would you describe the economic environment you grew up in. My dad Sol was a cab driver, my mom Claire worked for the state. We never wanted for anything but looking back, we sure weren't wealthy. Did you feel deprived, poor, middle class, wealthy?

COBHAM: I didn't want for money. For what? I did a gig with my father. He would pay me 50 cents. Fifty cents was off-the-hook. We had the greatest music in the world. AM Radio Top 10 pop music was Basie, Ellington, Brubeck. That is what they were playing. No such thing as FM at that time. Everything made sense. Harry James, Sinatra had hit records, Sarah Vaughan, Pops, Ella, an amazing eye opener. The esoteric side was Stan Kenton or Mingus. Every day. I didn't have any choice but to enjoy and absorb it. I did not hear Miles on that station. I would hear him on a show with Dr. Billy Taylor, very good piano player, who I ended up working with. 1010 was a music station. Dodger games on WNEW. The Giants on another station. Yankees on another. You listened to sports, news, and music. My Dad had a 1952 Chrysler in '53/'54. You could get a new Chrysler for fifteen hundred dollars

GRUBER: Were you an athletic kid? You said you played stickball. Were you any good?

COBHAM: No. Terrible. I got an occasional hit. But I was the smallest person on the street. They always gave me center field because it was the farthest place away.

I did go to Ebbets Field all the time with my dad. On a couple of occasions, we went to the Polo Grounds in the Bronx. It was like leaving and going to another country. To leave Bed-Stuy, to go to A&S to shop with my mother was like a big picnic. You went on the 'A' train from Utica Avenue to Hoyt and Schermerhorn 10 stops away and you were in another world. To go to 154th Street, the Polo Grounds? When you got home, "Wow, man, you went to see the Giants?! What are the people like up there?" It was a serious discussion for a week. "What kind of clothes did they wear?? Was it cold up there?" Don't even talk about Jersey - you are in a different galaxy.

As we wind down our conversation, I wonder how the process of selecting tunes will differ from, say, that of his last 10 shows.

COBHAM: Oh, this is different. For a big band, they are playing things...You know *Sal Si Puedes*, 'Get out if you can,' it's a musical labyrinth. I'm working with British musicians playing Latin music. That should be interesting. In the north, the approach is a duple form, *bup bup, bup bup, bup bup, bup bup*. The Latin form is triplets, *dadade dadade dadade dadade*. So (*scats the tune*), that's Latin. The challenge is to get these guys comfortable doing what they know is right for them through how I conduct them rhythmically. A lot of the material has a lot to do with cross-pollinating between the south and the north, and in the south, three is stronger than two. People walk in three. The Brazilian thing is *ba bo BA* (*scats*). When you see women, they are sort of sashaying on *1-2-3, 1-2-3, 1-2-3, 1-2-3*, a slower two. In the north, it is *1-2, 1-2, 1-2, 1-2*. That's how it sounds, how it feels. This is where the drums come in, they make you feel a certain way.

Saturday Morning Rehearsal, June 10, Bell Studios, Acton, London

I meet Mark Phinney in the anteroom lounge of the rehearsal space and we enter and quietly seat ourselves, with the band already in full tilt. I first met Mark on my home island of Koh Phangan, Thailand. He has flown halfway around the world for the prospect of shaking Bill's hand and a peek behind the scenes at rehearsals and shows. A concert and event impresario for decades back in the States, he is a true believer, a superfan with a sophisticated eye for detail both on the gear side and with the Cobham discography.

Guy Barker is conducting in an untucked white dress shirt, which ought to look disheveled, but instead adds a dashing aura of confidence and calmness. Confident and calm being the dominant attitudes of these 17 master musicians through the rehearsals, load-in and performances. Some artists achieve the distinction of maestro, fewer still earn a reputation as prolific maestro, across genres and platforms. Through the week, Guy will drop into other gigs, compose bits of a cello concerto and describe his work arranging music and performing in films like *The Talented Mr. Ripley*. He was a music director and arranger for the London Jazz Festival and for the BBC and has played with, well, everyone, earning him Member of the Most Excellent Order of the British Empire (MBE). So, he's chivalrous as well. Guy sports glasses, blue jeans and black shoes and paces often on the light hardwood floor.

To an outsider, the references to notations, chords and adjustments are an alien language but as the rehearsals progress, the logic and intentions become recognizable.

GUY BARKER: Why is that? That must be a mistake. Sorry. That's a Letter E...should we do the second part of the medley? The 'beastly' medley part two. BC medley. *Spectrum* and the *Funky Thide of Sings*...When we get to bar 21, saxophone, when we are in B and we have that phase, get rid of a beat there...*Here we go*...

COBHAM: Here we go…

Sheets of music lay scattered on the floor amidst a sea of stands. Silver cans of Diet Coke. A solitary coffee cup. The Bell Studios room presents exposed red brick walls, boasting meter-wide logos, and two venetian-blinded windows, one throwing shade, the second wide open. On my left are audio boards, set in hard orange cases. Large speakers hang from the wall by black chains.

Australian guitarist Carl Orr sits on the left side closest to the wall in a checkered short-sleeve shirt, studying his sheet music. He is playing a Lengardo Milano, a solid-body Les Paul-type guitar, sunburst mahogany body and neck with an ebony fingerboard and highly-figured maple cap on the front. Scottish keyboardist Steve Hamilton sits closer to the center in jeans and a black t-shirt, iPad mounted on a music stand. Steve has a band-aid on his right pinky; a purple folder lies next to him on the floor.

Bill sits in the center of the room against the wall. There is a long rectangular *Yamaha*-branded case, all-white drums, two music stands to his right. He wears a red long-sleeve shirt with French words spanning the center. To his left, filling out the rhythm section, is bassist Michael Mondesir, in jeans, black shoes, and black hat, his face lit by a near-constant smile. Carl, Steve, and Michael are longtime Cobham collaborators.

Sting Like a Bee

The Greenock Café, a short walk away, is offering a lunch special, cheeseburger, fries, and a Rio soft drink. Bill and I take the special, he insists on paying, but Mark orders only hash browns. Mark is not a shy eater but is experiencing a state of constant awe being in the presence of his lifelong musical hero, perhaps feeling a free burger procured from the maestro might offend as being *too much*.

Gnawing our way through our meals, Bill mentions the time he performed in a Broadway play with Muhammed Ali. *Wait, what?*

COBHAM: Muhammad Ali was the star - he put the money in it - and Oscar Brown Junior wrote the play (*starts singing the melody*). He was an actor (*sings some lyrics*), a playwright. I was the drummer in the band for the play. Two days after we started - we did it twice - we were shut down by Ed Sullivan.

GRUBER: Why did Ed Sullivan shut it down?

COBHAM: I don't know. He was a force on Broadway. He was writing for the *Daily News*. They just toed the line. He had a lot of clout.

GRUBER: Who told you it was Sullivan?

COBHAM: The director of the band. The musical director was a guy, played keyboards, from San Francisco, played in Jerry Garcia's band, black cat, really nice guy...MERL SAUNDERS! Merl was my guy, he hired me.

GRUBER: What was the name of the play?

COBHAM: *Big Time Buck White*. Look it up. Ali said, "You are in too good a shape. I'm going to show you what shape you're in." I said, "I'm good, show me what you got." He went from *here* (pointing to lowered right hand) to *here* to *here* and I never saw the hand move. All I felt was the wind...I had a stiff neck that day from that moment forward. Something hit me and I was on my ass. Whack! He went to grab my nose. He never punched you unless he had a clear shot. He slapped you, he stung you. It's like lightning going back up into the air after it struck the ground. He was amazing, man.

He said, "*float like a butterfly, sting like a bee.*" He said, "Bill, *sting*." That's how I learned how to play. I finally understood what (percussionist and prominent drum stick maker) Vic Firth was telling me by way of Muhammad Ali.

GRUBER: Sting the drums.

COBHAM: Draw the sound out. When he hit somebody, when he was setting them up, he kept stinging the surface. Look at Joe Frazier's face, man. Ali lost the first fight but the heavy was, Joe was in the hospital two weeks longer, just from being slapped.

GRUBER: The subject matter of the play was about race and oppression.

COBHAM: Yes, but hey. I was not into the subject matter of the play. Billy had a gig, working for Ali, I didn't give a *fuck* about the subject matter (*laughter at the table*). But it was wonderful, I had a ball. It was a great learning experience.

GRUBER: Ali and Martin Luther King, Jr. were called communists, were told 'you hate America.' The black power message was intimidating to people. Ali was attacked for being a draft dodger, a Black Muslim.

COBHAM: *Woooooh*, every negative name in the book. A socially negative minefield. The whole country. To this day.

Back in the rehearsal studio, I notice there is excellent, easy communication between Bill and Guy. This will not change in the course of the week.

BARKER: Top again. After you...

Guy is a confident, firm, but gentle bandleader, seamlessly volleying directions and changes with Bill. No arguments. Moving forward constantly. Band members speak openly about observations or issues, as changes are made on the fly.

Bill explains the meaning of *Sal Si Puedes*, an admonition to Panamanian slave laborers to '*Get out while you can*.' Then the two bandleaders talk and the horns come up.

They just keep playing, not much talking. During a trumpet solo, Mark mutters under his breath, "Powerful. Tight. Professional. Confident."

BARKER: Should I count it off?

COBHAM: Because I can't hear myself over the drums. Can we do four bars before...whatever...

BARKER: Play four bars. ONE, TWO...

They rehearse an ending again.

BARKER: OK, very good. Now can we go from, I would like to go...Yeah, that bar, we are going to do again...ahahah, I got it...let's go from letter K... we will leave that open here and I will cue the backings at B... one-two-eight ... hang on a second ... sorry ... *(clears throat)* ... let's do one more...shall we do the second part? ... *(laughter)*...when we get to bar 21...we should make exactly the same repeat...

COBHAM: What's he talking about? *Hahaha...*

At times, the rehearsal slips into a fast-moving cacophony of directions, riffs, sheet music alterations and band member chatter.

...bar 33, that break should be after two...really? ...it was the end of the tune? Right babeedleya ba boodeya, BOP... right at the very end, the very last... now at the top this, again, Bill sets it up... what you're saying is, until the bass comes in... you just do four bars... (hums the melody)... ready? ... here we go... Crosswinds... Stratus... Funky Thide of Sings... let's go back... 1-2-3-4-5-6... (sax solo)... yeah, that'll do it... alright, what are we on... what happens here, Billy is going to... and where the chart starts is... drum solo lead-in to 1, 2, 1, 2... drum solo...

Guy stands and leads but draws out information from Bill, who never seems attached to a particular idea or point of view, rather presents and shares then executes on what is directed. He laughs energetically at the end of most tunes.

BARKER: That's great guys... I'd say we should take a break? Want to do that? ... At least open the door to the other room...this old stuff...no, no, no... It goes... Yeah, let's do...try that again...we're not leaving till we get it right (*laughter*)... (*Carl plays rhythm riffs as the band laughs and chatters*) ... OK, then it's pretty much straight through. The thing is, just play it very lightly, very cool...

COBHAM: 1, 2, 1-2-3...(*music fills the room*).

BARKER: Guys, could we just do letter N to the end, Bill, tap just slightly slower, let's do it to the end...well done...that's it, that's it...Tomorrow...

After rehearsals, some of us gather at the neighborhood Bollo House pub. Over beers, Guy calls the gig a celebration of Bill's life and work in music. I ask him about his influences, the answer would take hours protests Barker, but he mentions Roy Eldridge, Lee Morgan. As a young man, he boasted 14 hours of Louis Armstrong VHS tapes, which he would watch at his apartment with Wynton Marsalis, Gil Evans, and other friends. Guy wanders over to the bar then returns, extending his phone to me. On the slightly cracked screen is a YouTube video of Leonard Bernstein conducting the New York Philharmonic, Louis honoring the great WC Handy by performing *St. Louis Blues*. Handy sits with his wife, and, mid-performance, begins to cry, taking a handkerchief from under his hat to wipe the tears streaming down his face. Bill and others look on. There is a rich legacy of great music performed and recorded for posterity. This week, the Guy Barker Big Band with Billy Cobham intends to add to it.

Sunday Morning Rehearsal, June 11, Bell Studios

The final day of rehearsal commences at 10am.

Guy gesticulates with his right hand, trumpet held in his left. He wears glasses but frequently removes and waves them while instructing musicians. Today it's a light blue shirt that's not tucked in to his jeans. He periodically walks back to the trumpet chair next to Michael Mondesir to play.

Bill's assistant/ intern/ surrogate son Santiago Roberts adjusts the drum kit as they play. At one point, he lies on the floor for an extended period holding an anvil against the bass drum. The band is all male. Bill laughs a lot. At 73, he seems to possess limitless energy. Easy trust is in the air.

BARKER: Letter Q... I'll cue Letter E a second time. You could have a bit longer there. It won't be too long... *(alto sax solo)* ... Bill will do four bars outside. Once you hear...

Next is *Stratus,* and the horns electrify the room. Mondesir is wearing dark glasses this Sunday morning, driving one of fusion's most recognizable and imitated bass lines. At the end, Guy says, "Perfect;" Bill deadpans, "That'll work."

Guy holds up his hand from the back of the room, "Let's start it again." He lifts his right hand and drops it sharply, *4, 3, 2, 1...*

Scattered around the studio floor are orange Bell Percussion coffee mugs. The coffee machine is an object of mystery. Looks easy enough, coffee packets on the left, selections on the right, pay, insert packet, but no one seems able to figure it out.

"Have you noticed how much they have tightened up today, last day before the gig?" Mark asks in a whisper. "Seriously tight. Bill moves effortlessly from Latin to funk and back again."

The rehearsal ends and musicians are given their instructions for Monday; they stream out with collegial goodbyes and see-you-tomorrows. Bill and I find seats on a sectional couch in the lounge to pick up on an earlier conversation.

GRUBER: At the end of today's rehearsal, you said you think you're almost there. What's not quite there?

COBHAM: I remember telling you a while back that, after the first day, I tend to not look at the music anymore. If you notice, I'm not looking at the music anymore. But I don't have it all together yet. It's lining things up a little bit more because I depend on being able to hear everybody in the band. Solos and everything. Problem with that is, I'm on the far side near the baritone saxophone player who has a solo and also plays piccolo. And in the middle of all that, *trombones* (*laughs*), and everything else. He's playing a piccolo part with the bass player who is right smack next to me so it's a problem of balance (*a trumpeter starts playing scales and patterns in the background*) and understanding the interactions in the arrangements as written. Guy has added a couple of bars here or there, maybe four bars in places where I would normally jump into things. So, I'm trying to separate the originals from the hybrid now. Interesting, sometimes.

GRUBER: Is it odd for you having composed this music to hear it coming through the eyes and ears of another composer?

COBHAM: Yeah sure, but at the same time I find myself a fan of it all. "Far out, I didn't think about it like *that*." That's where you want to be. You hear all the music written by Strayhorn and Duke and how people have taken that same music, with the same fundamental foundation, and, when you hear what they've done with it, you think, gosh man, it's a salute. Brings it to the forefront in another dimension. It's all a plus.

GRUBER: How often have you worked with someone who has arranged your music at this level of complexity?

COBHAM: Not often. Drummers are not 'musicians' normally so therefore they just keep time for musicians who don't have good time who supposedly write music. That's quite honest. In the world of jazz, drummers and singers are not musicians. They are the "drummers" and "singers."

GRUBER: How has the music progressed from yesterday to today?

COBHAM: Yesterday, we went through the whole thing with the idea of timing; if we can hear each other, we will be alright.

Guy comes by to report that a car will be at the studio shortly to pick Bill up, then goes over the critical details for opening day at Ronnie Scott's. "The Ibis car will turn up at two," says Guy, then instructs me with a smirk, "Make sure he is here for the car!" After a full day of rehearsal, Barker has another gig in a few hours. "Have a good concert tonight," offers Bill.

"Lunch at 12, two o'clock at Ronnie's." Guy confirms, as he heads out the front door, "Sound check at two, the band will all be there by four. We will do a quick sound check and we will all be ready."

GRUBER: What's it like for you to take direction from a bandleader? I assume during the show that he will be leading the band?

COBHAM: Yes, it's vital. It's either him or me. On some things, I am 'counting in.' On some things, I cannot, because, different tempo, people need to see one guy.

GRUBER: You will be focused on a different set of tasks.

COBHAM: The dynamics are the same. Once the tune starts, I control our destiny pretty much. Like in *Le Lis, To the Women in My Life*, normally in my quintet or sextet, everyone knows each other so well, they know what I am going to do. But we're talking about a 17-piece big band and I don't even know everyone's name. The wind player will say, 'just count it off' or 'give me a stick, so I have a shot.' In Ronnie's, if it is packed with people, it will absorb the high frequencies. If my voice is in the high or mid-frequencies, no one is going to hear it so easily. *ONE TWO THREE FOUR*. So, you come with a stick and go '*bop bop bop bop bop BANG*' where you can, various mechanisms, all about synchronization and timing. So, when we play in some situations and go back to *tempo primo*, everybody knows that (*scats several bars of the tune, then smacks hands together*). My band, they know it's going to be two beats, or at the beginning is one beat to come in at the new tempo. Here I have to go '*ah ah ah BANG,*' just to be sure. As soon as everybody gets comfortable, then we can get into the next level.

GRUBER: What will you be hoping to achieve tomorrow (Monday, first rehearsal at the club) afternoon that you didn't achieve today?

COBHAM: A balance of sound. We are building in the monitors. I'll have a wireless in my ears, and I want a balance of the whole band, especially soloists. When they get up and play in that soloist mic, I need to hear them, from the baritone sax to the trumpet.

GRUBER: Explain the importance of monitors.

COBHAM: A highly discriminative system where all you hear is what you need to hear to be comfortably part of the sonic environment. Just like if you are listening to a good piece of music at home. For me, I want to be able, for each tune, to understand the music the best I possibly can, so, if I am missing someone in the mix, I can fill it in in my head. I'm not at that point where I feel that comfortable yet. No matter how much you play in rehearsal…the (Michael) Jackson Victory tour rehearsed for six months before they even looked at a stage. The critics went, it was like robots on stage. You still have to go through those changes to get to the point where you are playing what you really mean. It's not 'rehearse' anymore, it's the next level. It's life.

GRUBER: When Guy threw out the letters N, R, Q…

COBHAM: Rehearsal letters. If you look on your music, you see a Section A; after a certain amount set of bars, you start B. (*I ask if all tunes start at 'A.'*) The melody could start at C after the introduction, until you get to the end of one of my tunes and you have A1 or Z2 (*laughs*), because the tune is long and they run out of the alphabet and start again.

GRUBER: How would you describe Guy's style as a bandleader? He seems to be very confident, chilled. At the pub last night, I mentioned to him my initial impression of the talent and respect and relaxed communication of the band members, and he used the word 'trust.'

COBHAM: Yes, go take a look at Leonard Bernstein conducting the *New York Philharmonic* with his face. He was amazing, man. You see someone who has arrived, where the tricks of his trade are inbred so everyone respects and trusts him. He will just look over at a section and they know exactly what to do. WC Handy, *St. Louis Blues*, he is conducting, but he wrote the arrangement, man. Guy wrote the arrangement, and when you write the arrangement, you are the arrangement.

GRUBER: You performed with Bernstein's Youth Orchestra.

COBHAM: 1961. Carnegie Hall. Watching what he did, how he conducted, how he transferred his thoughts through 100 people on stage, they all just functioned with him. That's magic. Same as with Miles, the body language. The fact that people like that tend to speak through their bodies, they don't talk a lot.

GRUBER: How did you qualify?

COBHAM: By being part of the School of Performing Arts. Think it was with Juilliard, Manhattan School of Music. We did *Carnival of the Animals*. I stood there petrified. To be in this guy's presence was daunting. Not intimidating on any level, but what he brought to the table was ridiculous.

GRUBER: You were 17?

COBHAM: I was 16. *West Side Story* premiered that year.

GRUBER: Was that an early example of fusion?

COBHAM: It was East Harlem, a deep Latin American environment at that time. East Side of Manhattan, 110th and 125th and Third Avenue going towards the East River. You couldn't call it *East Side Story*, didn't have the same feel (*laughs*). Fusion started in New Orleans, mixing in Latin rhythms. What (Bernstein) did, it made a lot of sense. That's an interesting question. Fusion, yeah, not much of a reach. A lot of great musicians played in that (*West Side Story*) band. Needed that jazz thing, people who could flow and be flexible.

GRUBER: Did you have any contact with Bernstein? Did you meet him?

COBHAM: I think he shook everybody's hand. Like the audience with the pope.

GRUBER: Living In New York. If you lived in Colon, or Springfield, Missouri, you might not have those experiences.

COBHAM: It's Mecca.

GRUBER: Can you recall anything you took away from that experience?

COBHAM: Ambition. A desire to study harder. I was chosen to go there. I was just a body. It was an honor to just be there. It did leave the residue of, do I want to do this or do I want to play more in the world? I wanted to make the transition to move from Latin to jazz to rock. I wanted to be a studio musician. I wanted to do what I saw my friend Keith's father Ray do. He did it all.

GRUBER: Guy's big band will showcase new arrangements of your work but you have worked with numerous classical and jazz orchestras in the past. When did you first become interested in working with an orchestra?

COBHAM: Started with Count Basie on the *Ed Sullivan Show* in 1952 on our black and white Crosley TV. My parents would call me when a drummer would come on. Sonny Payne would be the drummer with Basie. Belson with Basie or Ellington. And I would be inspired by them.

The drummer can be the leader in the orchestra. Even though the instrument appears to not sustain and control sounds in the way of intonation, it's not just the sound or the pitch, it's the personality and the way that the drum is played. What drummers tend to do is to sustain that feeling, a control, subtle but extremely strong. I wanted to learn how to do that.

If the drummer is very strong like Sonny Payne, bass, snare and floor tom, hi-hat and ride cymbal and a crash, and he pushed a 17-piece big band. The bass drum is so important in the big band because it supports the tonal quality to the bass and band by providing a percussive consistent rhythmic foundation. The drums, the bass, the rhythm guitar, these are the other frequencies that were missing. Then add the piano that plays the chords that help keep everyone synchronized. The rhythm section runs the band. Without that engine, there is no band. Take the guitar away and call it Oscar Peterson Trio, you have an engine that can outshine the Basie big band on a good day. Ray Brown, Ed Thigpen, you forget the Basie band is on the bandstand because it's that great. Oscar is creating in real time as he goes because he has that option and more musical latitude. Anything he plays will not be close to whatever he did before.

GRUBER: How does that work in a classical orchestra?

COBHAM: Fundamentally the same, Basie's big band and classical orchestra. They all have parts, they all need to know how to play those parts, with notations on a musical score called dynamics. The conductor has assigned everyone a purpose, play this part soft, crescendo this part, louder - ff - here or softer - pp - there. And he is directing people while they rehearse indications of where they need to be in real time on the stage while they are performing. That's what rehearsals are for.

GRUBER: Is it difficult for classical musicians in an orchestra who have not spent time with jazz to engage in an exercise like this?

COBHAM: Yes, because they have learned to play music in a specific way. They learned that repertoire. To improvise is an added dimension to their presentation. They never chose to go that route. They are in awe when they hear someone in their orchestra play a blues. Might just be a B flat chord, then you go to an E flat and then an F chord, you improvise and you tell a story only with the notes of those three chords, for instance. You are using those notes to connect and make a presentation, not so easy for those guys to do that until they have practiced doing it.

In a jazz orchestra, you play your heart, you interpret the music from your own perspective, it's more blue-collar. This is how I feel today, and these are the notes I will use to express how I feel today.

GRUBER: I heard Guy saying he took Jan Hammer's improvisations...

COBHAM: He took Jan's solos on parts of *Crosswinds* but he combined it with the original solo from George Duke. Then he took more of Jan's solo on *Stratus*.

GRUBER: Is there an opportunity to repurpose the arrangements and use them again?

COBHAM: They are mine and I can do whatever I want with them. It's an investment on my part to open up another world. What I am providing is something commercially viable. I'm looking to get people up standing up, clapping, enjoying it, to 17-22 pieces. Think of my idea as an extension of Tower of Power - about 10 pieces - with the same foundational groove mindset. Someone wants to write my music in symphony, I might even invest in that. Could be a way to open doors that are otherwise closed. There has got to be another way to work than just playing clubs. But it begins with believing in oneself and pursuing your dream to make it a reality.

GRUBER: Do you have other arrangements of your compositions written by someone else?

COBHAM: From Scott Stroman. I worked with the London Jazz Orchestra in 1998. As matter of fact, the trumpet player who walked out just now, he was in that band. In 2000, we worked on the road in Europe with that orchestra.

At which point, Bill declares it's two o'clock, 'we gotta shut down,' and he takes his final leave of the Bell rehearsal space. Tomorrow is showtime. I encourage Bill to get a good rest and he confirms that we will pick up our conversation at lunchtime tomorrow.

Ronnie Scott's, Monday Mid-Afternoon, Load-In

At 2pm, Ronnie Scott's is quiet as an empty church. Gradually the space is filled with more people, more gear, more hustle.

(Drilling) Two club techs respond to requests from Bill. "If you could find an adapter, I need to power up this thing." He taps a snare drum three times. "Go ahead, it'll work, it'll work. There's no legs for the floor tom?"

With Santiago, the venue techs Chris and Charlie and band members all working on load-in, Bill's voice is the most active, he is in perpetual physical motion, instructing, requesting, imploring with a *please* and *thank you*.

GRUBER: What is the load-in process for you?

COBHAM: When I worked with Mahavishnu, I always loved to be able to go after my gear was set up and lose myself in it. This was my way of coming to grips with what I had to do later on that day. It was a private time for me. To address my weaknesses as a player. I played patterns, to be consistent. I would focus on a lot of different things, one being my posture, which was poor. I watched a lot of musicians who sat below the drum set, conceding their power for the way they looked in performance. They would have to raise their hands and elbows above their shoulders to play the cymbals and, in this action, concede power generated from the center of their body. I realized, how about if I sat at an equal level as if the drum set was a table for breakfast or dinner. And I would scoop out of the bowls or select parts of the day's menu with my eating utensils, as if I was having a good meal. Everyone could see me better and my performance was more focused on the core source of my power. I could reach out more effectively to achieve anything I wanted from the musical palette that is my drum set.

…I knew it was too good to be true…the problem is that…I can't believe it. All of them are gone. We had all the tom-tom legs together…can you do me a favor? I just need something to plug it in. This works…it's over here…GOT IT! Yeah, much better!…(drilling)…I would never have done that. They are very special…OK, cool…it looks like I have to go with…it's a TAMA…DHL from Jeremy…somewhere between Swiss and Germany, because it came from my house…it was supposed to go in the trap case or with the toms in the tom case…do they have a London office? A British office…(Bill cackles).

GRUBER: You could play a few recognizable hits and a few jazz standards and 90 percent of people coming out for a night of entertainment might not notice. What motivates you at this point in your life to work as hard as you do and to create new music?

COBHAM: I don't consider what I do as work. It is for me more about the objective, my gift, which is to perform and play. Whatever it takes for me to be on the bandstand, if I am enjoying myself, it is well worth the input and effort to make it happen.

GRUBER: You talked about the stamina you developed in the army. Were you physically fit as a young man before the army, was that always a part of your makeup?

COBHAM: Yes sir, all of my family. We didn't smoke, drink alcohol, didn't do drugs. I didn't believe in having any drug that could incapacitate me.

GRUBER: Your cousin Edwin is a religious man, was that a theme in your family life, church-going, not getting involved in substance abuse?

COBHAM: We were Methodists. I ran track for high school, was a catcher playing baseball. Edwin played football in Panama. He went to the Merchant Marine Academy, had to be in shape. A ship's pilot has to jump off a ship.

GRUBER: Yes, I know, I did it with him.

COBHAM: You don't do that if you can't make it.

GRUBER: It was midnight, we were on a small, fast boat in the Panama Canal, when I notice this ladder over the side of a huge Ukrainian cargo ship. Edwin is boasting about how he works out so that he can catch the ladder. Next thing I know he jumps off the boat and I realize I'm next.

I ask Bill for the final playlist as the background chatter intensifies.

COBHAM: 10 pieces. The compositions are: *Cap Breton, a medley of Stratus, Light at the End of the Tunnel and Crosswinds, Eggshells Still on My Head, Obliquely Speaking, To the Women in My Life/ Le Lis, Two for Juan, Sal Si Puedes, Red Baron.*

I need for, 18 and 16...give me, that's 15, 13... (drum roll) ...(drilling)...ah, I see what, like this...12, 10...we have another issue...this guy won't work with this guy...you don't need that...somebody did something... is there another rack? Take one away...Put the five and a half in, put the other one away. Is that a six?... Use that as a back up...just take off...(drilling) ...(trumpet scales are played in the distance)...

GRUBER: If, say, a music professor watches the show over the next six nights, would they see an evolution? For a lot of bands, each night is the same show, another gig.

COBHAM: Guar-UN-teed as Alvin Batiste used to say. Every night is going to be a whole *'nuther thang*. As we play, we grow. We build upon the night before. We are projecting 90 minutes of material that is rocking for 17 pieces.

GRUBER: What are you expecting from your rhythm section for this run? Are they doing something different here? You rehearsed with them before bringing in the horns.

COBHAM: Carl, solid support as a mostly rhythm guitarist, locked in there. He provides a groove. Steve, very supportive in terms of the sections foundation, *grand pianoforte* on all levels. Mike, strong stalwart energy force, very consistent. Unique in what he does, once he is comfortable, he is like the Rock of Gibraltar. The rhythm section focus is for everyone to be on the same page at all times.

GRUBER: How do you use time off between shows in a run of six days?

COBHAM: It's important for me to be very private. With my wife, in my personal cocoon, with my closest friends, act like it's an everyday thing. A little time to rest and, oh by the way, I play a concert in the evening. My actions offstage should reflect the Sly Stone label. *Everyday People.*

More musicians are arriving, greeting each other, gathering in pairs and small groups, laughing, gossiping.

GRUBER: So, what was that with the toms before, just some high-level management resolution I overheard?

COBHAM: Yeah, it's done. It's coming from Birmingham but we'll get here.

GRUBER: Really? From Birmingham *(calculating hours to show time)*?

COBHAM: Yeah. Alabama. JUST JOKING!!!

(Directing the crew) Grab this, take that...I'm not going to use the wood one...see if they've got, just let me borrow... I need to use a Yamaha floor tom...we played that years ago...no problem, a little bit, happy... Charlie? ...don't give him any ideas (laughter)...It's gotta hit right straight up on it, no no, my fault... (several taps on a drum) ...Yeah, there you go. That'll get it for tonight anyway...Mark, so how's life, man?

Mark responds, "I'm learning a lot..."

COBHAM: So am I. It never ends...I need a C... AAAH! An interesting note. Painful, but...I'll show you what I am going to do...*Get out of me way*...There, right? So, if we did something like this *(Bill demonstrates a military roll)*, I need to raise the crazy angle of the bass drums up on the mounts. It should be about here, or here?... Angle them up so it should be just like that, the sound should be just like that...that's cool... *(Bill plays soft to strong, fast to slow)* ...It's a lot better than it was, now I still have to pull this back to get those hi-hats in... OK, just pull the whole thing back, can you, that's where I want to be...

Guy is setting places for each of the band members on the stage. Not everyone will fit, so it's tricky. "I'll be here. Not ideal, but..." (Bill sings in the background).

COBHAM: There's nothing you can do? Surely, there is something we can do. The ride...now you know, bring it forward... Is there any way to move that to your left? The whole stand. Thanks, man. Every little bit helps. Raise it up here. Keep it there. Now tighten it. OK, there it is! ...Teamwork. Two of 'em? There was another soft case. Was there anything in it?... Put that one...That'll get it... Give me the smaller one. And I'll put the triangle on the right-hand side... *(Bill tests the new range of drums).*

(Sound of cymbals) ... you'll put that one there...this one here...this is my second ride...we've got to turn it around because it's not working, turn it the other way...no, no, no... there it is, there it is...now pull it back...now raise it...now if you can pull the whole stand in more, it will work, thanks, angle it down a little bit...well, it was an idea... Let's try the other one...I think it's a little too brass... (Bill plays the drums) ...that's really nice... I think I'm OK... (hits three cymbals) ... Charlie, I make it nine channels drums...I'm up there...I never said so, I just got up and... wonderful, I need more...very exciting...me? Music stand?... Now? Now? No. Now? No.... (sound of percussion as each of Bill's instruments are tested) ... I need those heads now please. Maybe we can get some of them on. 12, 13, 14, 15...(drilling)...

BARKER: Look at all the room we have!

Each inch of space is carefully managed. Real estate is at a premium with 17 musicians and gear on a stage built for half that. An alto sax begins playing in a corner of the club. Most of the band have arrived, camping in corners and tables around the room. The place is buzzing with activity and sound. No one is anxious, there are no disagreements, no harsh words. I ask Bill to narrate what he is doing.

COBHAM: I am just tuning heads, changing the drum heads, so it suits, more to my liking, what I think the band will sound like in this room. Synthetic calf hide, if you will. Evans old '56 line, commemorating their anniversary. I think Wyatt Earp was still around at the time. You never know.

> *At rehearsal, he carries with absolute clarity the direction we will go artistically. As for the rhythm section, he is the king, the tiger, as I say, from his 'office;' he controls everything, but at the same time he is listening and feeling everything. He makes the rhythm and uses the drums in a melodic way, controlling the tonality of each drum. What really draws my attention is that he is always willing to take risks of all kinds; in a small club or a big televised concert, that adrenaline makes his music*

have blood. And this makes attending one of his concerts a unique and unrepeatable experience.

-- Christian Galvez, Chilean bassist, frequent Cobham band member

Steve Hamilton notices that the keyboard rental is the same one he used in the last gig. It still has all his 'stuff' on it from last time. I ask if that will be useful at all. "Very useful, yeah, saves me from having to set it all up again."

Mark is rattling off observations next to me. I ask him to describe what he sees.

PHINNEY: We have five chairs upfront (saxophones), each chair is mic'd with an SM58 Shure, industry standard, everybody uses those. Second row, four chairs (trombones), three microphones. In the back row for the trumpets they have cigar mics, also unidirectional drum-style mics. Only two for four players. Strange, almost a hybrid of a cocktail kit and a rock and roll concert kit. Two floor toms and seven raised toms. Two snares, might be a piccolo snare. Standard 8-inch snare. Can't imagine they are micing the drums. I guess people are going to be using in-ear monitors.

GRUBER: You are surprised how involved Bill is in the set up.

PHINNEY: I have never seen a rock drummer do anything. Bill at his age lifting toms, adjusting toms, removing his own heads with a drill, basically doing most of the work. I am really surprised. It's a lot of work. It's going to take him two hours to set this up. Bending, lifting, moving back and forth.

I ask why he thinks Bill does it.

PHINNEY: He wants everything just right. This is an engineering project. It's like building a building. Pretty tricky. A lot of factors. Space not the least of which. You will never see a kit like this in a regular jazz band. This is a full-on rock and roll concert arena kit.

GRUBER: What's the difference?

PHINNEY: Rock drummers play really loud because they have to keep up with the guitar players. They like big toms, usually big, thick, deep snares. It has to be louder and bigger. A jazz trio, you wear a suit and a tie, you maybe use a three-piece kit. But they are doing everything in this project. Powerful fusion stuff, powerful jazz but at the same time bring it down real low to do some beautiful stuff too. So, he has got a kit that can do it all.

Soundcheck

The band is in place for the soundcheck and Guy Barker is holding court. He asks the band to play something and, obliging, they play for a few seconds.

COBHAM: OK, what I need from you, Carl, is, can you tighten up the articulation a little, I hear the top end OK, the high-mids are kind of strange. Try it again, play the solo...*1, 2...*

As Carl plays, a tech asks over the PA, "Everyone on the rhythm section, are you all good for your ears for now? Wonderful."

BARKER: We will just do a couple of things. Can we do *Obliquely* please? As written, just exactly what is on the...Here we go, 1-2-3-4. *(Horns come up)* ... Letter B, what we rehearsed. 1, 2, 3, 4...Opening again.

COBHAM: *(Shouting) 1, 2, 3, 4*...Yeah, but hold on. May I have, I need more keyboards, a little bit more guitar, if you have my drums in the mix, take them out, I have more than I need...

BARKER: Can we go from bar 23, here we go, *1, 2, 3...*

COBHAM: *1-2, 1-2-3... (horns come up) ...*

BARKER: This is Letter R... I'll give you, two bars in, Letter R...three times 'round...trombones, you should be marked *third time only*, and so you only play the last line, the third time...OK, same place, here we go...*1,2...*so what I'll do, you got 16 bars, once we hit that *babadee babadoo . . .*

COBHAM: That part's OK. You can just cue me in. You guys ready? Want me to start? Is it only me?

BARKER: Let's go from the top again.

COBHAM: *1, 2, ah, ah, ah, ah...*

BARKER: Let's do that again. Letter G... 47? ...*1-2-, 1-2-3*...Something happened there... when they play the figure in 58, we lost a beat somewhere...it's cool, it will be fine tonight...How does everybody feel? ... Do you have any questions on that? Does it all make sense?

COBHAM: Of course not. Before next year, we'll figure it out.

BARKER: We'll do it again tomorrow...this is more medium tempo...solo, and then...you should have them...so again, this starts...count in to bar 10 and the rhythm section starts...open piano solo...after you, Bill...the melody starts on the second bar for me...the rehearsal letter is in the wrong place...one bar later...oh, really...top again...

And then, after days of rehearsal, they're as ready as they're going to be.

Showtime, Opening Night, June 12th

A chalkboard in front of Ronnie Scott's artfully presents the 17 members of the band.

Billy Cobham	Drums
Guy Barker	MD/ Trumpet
Nathan Bray, Tom Rees Roberts, Andy Greenwood	Trumpets
Barnaby Dickinson, Alister White, Winston Rollins	Trombones
Mark Frost	Bass Trombone
Nigel Hitchcock	1st Alto Sax
Sam Mayne	2nd Alto Sax
Graeme Blevins	1st Tenor Sax
Paul Booth	2nd Tenor Sax
Phil Todd	Baritone Sax
Steve Hamilton	Keys
Carl Orr	Guitar
Michael Mondesir	Bass

The club's 220 seats are sold out for the week. Mark describes the pre-show scene, as the lights are lowered and guests are seated for dinner and drinks as a *'quiet quivering pool of water.'* Expectant, excited, imminent. The club's history tracks Bill's musical life, if you include his drum and bugle corps youth. The black and white photos of jazz icons that line the walls claim at most one degree of separation; Bill has either played with everyone featured or played with someone who played with them. Same with tonight's patrons and musicians. Between Bill and Guy - and band members who regularly play the club - tonight's patrons own a degree of familiarity with the talent about to occupy the stage.

At 8:15pm, Ronnie Scott's stylish impresario and managing director Simon Cooke ambles up to the microphone in brown leather boots, a light summer coat, a dark open-necked shirt and blue jeans. According to co-owner Michael Watt, the business was in a shambles before Cooke "shaped the place up." To the uninitiated, this is a routine intro but that belies the intimacy of a decade-long relationship - five decades if you go back to the 1968 Horace Silver show - and the importance of setting the stage. In under a hundred words, Cooke instructs the audience. That they should be excited. That what they are about to see is special. That they are seeing one of the greats. That the club values its relationship with Cobham. And that they are damn lucky to have their seat because it's a sellout. The crowd hushes as Cooke takes the microphone.

> *A wonderful week ahead of us. It's completely sold out. Featuring a great collaboration between Guy Barker up there on the trumpet (applause) and this wonderful big band, who are all resplendent before you, and with one of the great jazz drummers, a real figure in history at Ronnie Scott's, and a massive figure in the history and the ongoing story of jazz, ladies and gentlemen please welcome to the stage the Guy Barker Big Band with...MISTER BILLY COBHAM!!!*

After introducing the band, Simon spends a good part of the show between the bar and the room's entryway with music critic Mike Hobart of the *Financial Times*. An accomplished musician and bandleader in his own right, Mike has reviewed and interviewed Bill for the *FT* in the past and seems to be enjoying the show.

> *The evening opened with shimmers of fanfare brass answered by swirls of mellow reeds and Billy Cobham quietly marking the pulse with sparse cymbal splashes.*

> *Then a firm Cobham count cued a salvo of brass; a quick rat-a-tat signalled a swaggering bass guitar riff; and Cobham kicked in with his trademark groove...* [2]

The Fan

The club's front of house staff places me at the bar for the week, so as to stay out of the paid seats and stay out of trouble. It's a fantastic view, back of a small club, straight-ahead look at the stage with superb acoustics. No photos are permitted, but Simon Cooke allows me to shoot pictures for the first two songs of the show, using Bill's cannon-like Leica. Bill's photographic work has been featured in numerous exhibitions and he programs the camera for my idiot-proof use. *Touch here, don't touch that, use this button like so.*

Throughout the opening night show, a blonde, thirty-something woman on the barstool to my right is moving feverishly to the music and cheerleading the band. Her enthusiasm infects everyone at the bar. That night, I tag Bill's Facebook page with some photos. I get an immediate response from Leya Jane Moore.

> *Hi Brian! I was the lass sat next to you and dancing all night! I was rather in ecstasy. Like watching something spiritual and magical and strong and voodoo and clear and tight and alive and actually, just very bloody shit hot!*

> *Both my parents were huge fans of Billy Cobham. My dad was a drummer, in a jazz funk band. Billy was his ultimate drummer. He and my mum saw the Mahavishnu Orchestra live in 1973, when mum was pregnant with my older brother. It was while leaving the gig that they decided to call my brother Jan, after Jan Hammer.*

> *Crosswinds was played to me from the crib, up. Many a time, I would walk into a room and find Dad meditating to You Know, You Know. Cobham's athleticism and zen-like light touch has been a constant. It's my power music. When I need to think - Crosswinds. When the world gets a bit over-complicated and I need perspective - Pleasant Pheasant. My dad had passed away and I was approaching*

---

[2] Hobart, Mike. "Billy Cobham with the Guy Barker Big Band, Ronnie Scott's, London — technically superb." *Financial Times*. June 13, 2017.

my '40s; I entered a competition on Facebook to win tickets. All I had to do was name my favourite song of his, Pleasant Pheasant...and I won! Like an otherworldly birthday present from my dad and the perfect way to celebrate. More totally and utterly amazing a show I have not seen. The power! The playfulness! The lightning reaction cymbals! I had to raise my eyes up and say, "Thank you!"

2 KIDS

It's Tuesday afternoon and Soho's streets are invaded by an army of ecstatic 10-year-olds.

> *On June 13th, 2017, the Ronnie Scott's Charitable Foundation invited legendary drummer Billy Cobham to take part in a workshop involving a local primary school, the Soho Parish Primary School. Pete Letanka, a jazz pianist/educator worked closely with the Foundation to give children the chance to perform and compose in the style of internationally renowned drummer Billy Cobham. Billy himself worked with the kids and joined them in a performance at Ronnie's.*
>
> *-- Ronnie Scott's press release*

Down the narrow Frith Street sidewalk leading to Ronnie's, kids in neon yellow-striped vests are marching, skipping, walking in stride, big wide eyes. It's a field trip! Out of school and out into the adult world. Teachers and aides are busily directing, herding, communicating, with parents acting as street crossing guards. Once the kids get to the venue, they try to peek in, try to see what's going on in this magical grown-up land of music, booze and late-night entertainment. Looks fancy! Parents are talking into iPhones as if military radios, giving and taking serious-sounding instructions, breaking into smiles when their kids come into view. It's a summer day, warm by London standards, so there is a mix of shorts and jackets as if not trusting the sunshine. Some parents hold small coats folded over a forearm.

Just in case. Some kids seem shy, most are expectant. There's a non-stop stream of kids chattering and waving of hands.

Once in, they are agog at the adult stuff, scanning the walls for clues of what goes on in forbidden places. The young performers assemble on stage and seem remarkably prepared, settling in to prearranged spots. Some are squatting, most standing, some seeming perfectly at home, some awestruck and trying to make sense of it all.

Pete Letanka is setting up his mic stand in front of the keyboard he'll be using to orchestrate. The room is starting to fill and the kids on stage adjust body language as it slowly sinks in that they are the entertainment, that they have something to deliver, live, in front of an expectant audience. It's showtime! Some kids in the audience lean forward, waiting, heads on splayed stacked hands. Moms are taking off jackets (they're still kids after all) as the kids wonder, am I supposed to break loose here or behave? What are the rules? Who enforces them?

A row of seven kids now forms in front with a colorful variety of xylophones. Simon Cooke emerges from backstage, two buttons open on his white shirt, eyeglasses hanging from a third, with Bill trailing in black T-shirt, as bandleader/ instructor/ event organizer Pete Letanka's voice comes over the PA. "Hello everybody. This day gets more and more surreal as it goes on." Peter wears a black shirt with rolled-up sleeves and red tie, and, grasping the mic with his right hand, asks, "Have you seen that movie *Bugsy Malone*?" A loud round of primary-schooler *yeses* and *yeahs* spill from the crowd. Parents apparently get that they should be quiet. It's the kids' gig.

"*Bugsy Malone* is like a wicked movie because it's basically about kids doing grown-up things, driving cars, wearing suits, and it's surreal to turn around and look, here we are, in this incredible place, Ronnie Scott's, right here in the heart of Soho." Pete has spent six days working with these year-six kids; they have written all the music and lyrics together. He declares, "If you know these kids, they look sweet, but they're *bossy!*"

Upon being introduced, Bill throws his hands in the air, dancing a jig, kicking his feet way out. Pete says, "All of the music has been inspired by this man." They've been listening to Bill's music for a week and wrote their own based on what they heard.

Bill confesses, "I cheated, I rehearsed with the band. They brought tears to my eyes, couldn't believe what they did. We are just going to show you and then you'll understand what music can do." He takes his seat behind his drum set to the sound of over a hundred 10-year-olds cheering wildly. "Here we go."

The kids are using a variety of percussion instruments – Bill told the kids to bring their pots and pans and five pounds for the school event earlier in the day - and Bill is having a great time, slipping often into a beatific, proud expression. Pete's keyboards guide the songs forward. There are seven in the front row, another seven in the second, then a group of four and finally a row with three violins and a sax. That last row gets up dramatically mid-song to join the performance. The tune starts out a little rough, though charming, and gradually gets tighter. Expressions vary - from laughing and smiling ear-to-ear to serious concentration - with frequent sideways glances to see that they are in step, or simply to see that they are being seen. Cobham is driving the beat, gently in the background though energetically during bridges.

Pete introduces a second tune, "We start this piece with these extraordinary solos." One girl forgets her line midway, while a girl with glasses next to her peers out into the audience, perhaps scanning for mom or dad. "Take it to the sky now…" Bill is taking it all in, watching as the kids use choreographed in-unison arm gestures, pointing out to the crowd, folding arms, pointing back at him.

By the third song, they are looking like they belong here, comfortable, focused on their instruments and cues, banging on a range of instruments, some perhaps homemade.

Pete then gives a primer on time signatures. "Nice cup-of-tea, nice cup-of-tea," then folds his arms and asks the kids and parents to do the same. "Here we go, now let's see if you can do it four times." He smacks his thighs standing up, "When I am doing like *this*, I am doing two things. With this hand I am doing 1-2-3, 1-2-3, 1-2-3, and with the other hand, 1-2-3-4, 1-2-3-4, and we suddenly have two rhythms going across each other and that is the starting point of our brand-new composition, *Time Divider, Three*

Against Two." The kids then deliver their original musical exploration of time signatures.

Pete masterfully manages respect for the kids as proper performers while allowing that they are kids. The quality of their performing, amidst some out-of-key moments and botched vocal solos, is surprisingly good. They have the confidence of kids taught by skilled teachers, in a safe and encouraging environment.

For the finale, the kids all stand as an electric bass guitar is added in the back. The song title is *Billy Cobham* and there's a dramatic a capella break with the audience clapping along and cheering. Hands pointing "up to the sky." I'm walking around video recording much of it on my iPhone and, being a sap, what can I say, I tear up often. It's very heartwarming stuff.

> *He can shake the time,*
> *Make this music mine.*
> *Keep us all in line,*
> *Watch us shine.*

Pete has them end with three big bows in unison then gives them a double thumbs-up. He turns the mic over to Bill.

"Education is very important, here's a great model right here." He tells them he would like to put them in his pocket and take them all over the world to tour with him. "When I was a little person like you, wow, I was lucky enough to go to the School for Performing Arts. I had to prepare for it. You are doing exactly what me and my buddies did to prepare."

I ask Pete for a run-down after the event. He says the class is a mixture of ten- and eleven-year-olds. It was a long-held dream of his to bring children to perform at Ronnie Scott's with a major artist. He was still processing what just happened.

LETANKA: The process was extremely organic, a real unfolding of ideas. It was amazing to see the growing confidence in these young people over the course of six days. Some children who I could barely hear answer their names are suddenly singing a solo in front of a jazz legend. The kid who really struggles to concentrate is suddenly the most focused kid in the room. And amazing to witness the moment when an uncertain hand is raised and a child asks if what they're about to sing might be any good for a chorus. Then what they sing is ultimately performed on stage at the legendary Ronnie Scott's jazz club. Extraordinary, really!

I think the thing that moves me the most though is looking up during the performance to see twenty-five kids really concentrating and putting everything they've got in this one moment, and then looking over to see Billy Cobham really concentrating and putting everything he's got in this one moment. It's a reminder of the meritocracy of music. Any difference falls away and for that moment we are all simply musicians.

A young female reporter interviews Bill backstage after the Soho school performance.

REPORTER: You're a very influential musician, *Rolling Stone* greatest drummers, what was it like to work with the kids?

COBHAM: Well it surprised me. You might know Francois Truffaut, a French movie director. He made a movie called *Small Change*, so good. It was about little people like this who were going to grow up and they already had their ideas of who they wanted to be. It's exactly them. They are only 6, 7, 8, 9, 10 years old, speaking what they believe to be *maturely*. You hear these little voices. I remember those days.

I had a very close friend who passed away, Keith Copeland. Didn't know we were both interested in music. Until one day, he said, man I have to go home. I thought we were going to play stickball. He said, "My father just bought me a drum set." I said, "What, really??" I think I was nine. "Can I come and see?" He said, "Yeah, come on over. Ronnie Bedford will be the teacher." I found out who Bedford was, played with all these amazing musicians, played in a band called Johnny Richards' orchestra. Richards arranged for Bob Hope, Stan Kenton. And, of course, with Keith's father Ray Copeland, legendary trumpet player who performed with people like Thelonious Monk and Charles Mingus. I walked in and saw the drum set and I said, "*Geez*," and just what this wonderful young (Soho) teacher said about playing three against two, that was the lesson that Ronnie Bedford was teaching. It just brought back all these memories. He said, (*Bill taps out*)

1-2-3, 1-2-3, 1, 2, and this is how you have to play it. It was just in the very beginning of the popularity of a man by the name of Dave Brubeck, who wrote *Take 5*, and it was all odd meters (*demonstrates with his hands and voice*). This was going on. I had no idea, I thought I'll never be able to play that. Wow, I thought, maybe my folks will get me a drum kit someday. When I got in to the School of Performing Arts, that was my gift. We went all the way to 2014 and then Keith passed away. And guess what? Keith still had his drum set. And now it's mine, because his wife gave it to me, "This is from Keith."

There is a knock on the door. A woman comes in and asks, can we take a quick picture with the kids? The reporter inquires if she can ask one last thing.

REPORTER: Do you think the kids taught you anything?

COBHAM: They didn't teach me anything but they gave me faith. That there is a future. And they are it.

Bill goes out to take photos with the kids, vamping for the camera, laughing, the kids loving it, validated, full of joy. Now that it's over, no more serious, focused looks. They're just kids.

From an interview with Ronan Guil, February 2014, one year before Keith Copeland's passing.

> KEITH COPELAND: *So, I had two cymbals, a rack tom, bass drum, snare drum, hi-hats. I worked with that a long time and I think the last thing that I got was a floor tom to complete the set. I bought that myself because I had a little paper route. I was delivering newspapers. I saved up enough money to buy me a floor tom...I was about 13 by the time I got the whole set. I was practicing and playing. And Billy Cobham lived in my neighborhood at that time. He was from Panama. We went to the same Junior High School. And I remember I got my whole set before Billy Cobham got his whole set. So, he'd come over my house and play. He always had great chops.*
>
> RONAN GUIL: *Even from the beginning?*

COPELAND: Yeah, because he used to play in the St. Clement's Catholic Church drum corp. He played the tenor drum because there were three girls that were fantastic snare drummers. They wouldn't let him play snare drum because his chops weren't good enough, so that was his incentive to really work on his chops. He'd come over and play on my set. And we'd have little battles on my drum set to see who could outplay each other... he was about 15...[3]

GRUBER: Was there a point where your father tried to inculcate the love of music or jazz or musicianship in you?

COBHAM: If he did, it was very slick. Because I didn't know it. We would go to dances or a rehearsal and he would just do these things. It always triggered a positive response. People acknowledged him, and me, for this positive thing he was doing; I wanted to do the same thing. I loved the music. As long as it was played with heart and feeling, I was enthralled by it. When I listened to classical music, it was the same way.

GRUBER: Did your mom have a similar love of music?

COBHAM: Mom loved music but she was more comfortable being housewife and controller of our home environment. Had everything worked out better as a family, you would have found her at home. She was a tailor, very creative, she would make patterns for people, with images from an *Amsterdam News*, a *Daily Mirror*, *Daily News*, and her payment was to see her work walking down the street.

GRUBER: At some point, I would love the technical details of Keith's first drum set.

COBHAM: I'll tell you right now. It's a 22-inch bass drum, a 5½ by 14-inch snare drum, 8 by 12-inch rack tom. Two 16-inch floor toms. All the old trappings. I'm having my guys cleaning that stuff up. All of the heads are original. Still says Manny's Music Shop, 48th Street. When I saw the drum set, I was shocked, in drum heaven. For some reason, it started to take hold on me. It was the first time I reached out and touched a drum set and heard it live.

---

[3] Guil, Ronan. "Conversations with Mr. KC." *Mostly Music*. February 2014.

GRUBER: When did you start taking lessons?

COBHAM: If I have studied with or been in the presence of more than five teachers in my life, that's a lot. My father took me to see Specs Powell, drummer in *West Side Story* on Broadway. Next time was Warren Smith, worked with Gil Evans. It did move me in the direction I wanted to go, jack of all trades. Then the great Chauncey Morehouse, who played bass drum in the New York Philharmonic. I was still leaning toward classical percussion but it didn't last very long. After that, my biggest teachers were drum and bugle corps marching band teachers, of which there were two. Bobby Thompson. And Ken Lemley, who showed me the way with rudiments. After that I taught myself. And watching the greats on TV, in real life, playing, Max Roach, Buddy.

I went to Music and Art High School, northernmost part of Manhattan, Compton Avenue and 135th Street. Many artists, much of the band Blood, Sweat & Tears came out of that school. Laura Nyro, one or two years after me, Janis Ian was in school with me. Eddie Gomez, the bass player, sat next to me in my home room class. The great Jimmie Owens, trumpet player, Larry Willis, who played with Harry Belafonte. (New York City Mayor) Fiorello LaGuardia started the school in the '30s I think. Because Roy Haynes and Ray Copeland recommended that I should take the examination, they thought I had good ears and a good sense of rhythm, I ended up going for three years, '59 to the summer of '62.

GRUBER: And a couple of years later, you were in the army. Were you concerned about being drafted?

COBHAM: My number was up. I knew it was coming. I was playing the 168th Street Armory up in the Bronx and I was in a band run by a guy named Ron Anderson. One of the things I learned was, if I am on time, and played well, and I don't cause anybody any problems, the chances are I would get hired again. I know I need to get to the gig first so I can be ready. If it's an hour set-up, be there early, then leave a half-hour or hour after the band leaves to tear it down myself.

That is when I met Hendrix. I remembered him because he played upside down guitar. He had moves that would not quit. Great rhythm player. I would play dances at the *Armory*, had a 220-yard indoor track, huge place, collegiate athletics all the time in the winter.

GRUBER: What do you remember about playing the gig with him? Do you remember what he looked like, what he was wearing? And what were you playing? Rock? Jazz? R&B?

COBHAM: White shirt, black pants. Might have been Marcel-processed hair to be slicked down. R&B definitely. It was about people dancing.

GRUBER: In watching you over the years, and watching older videos, there is an incredible physicality that you bring. When you talk about the drum and bugle corps, was there something about that approach that affected your playing, your physical sense of style?

COBHAM: Yes, it was the discipline of playing with others, so that we sounded like one drummer playing. The objective was to play as part of a unit and to make all the drums together sound alike. Look and sound exactly like your colleagues, the same patterns. If you can do that, you could win the contest. This instilled in me a tremendous amount of discipline, to be observant and to practice in a specific way, to develop a routine, to watch myself in a mirror so as to sharpen my skills. To watch how my sticks went up and down.

The strokes had to be as close to being the same as possible. I never started with sticks touching the head. A half-inch above the head, stroke the head. This is how I practice everything, to this day. Since this is such a demanding physical instrument, how can I pace myself over time to be effective at a high proficiency level. Controlling the power. Understanding where the power emanates from, setting the body. How to draw the sound out of each instrument. How can I be creative in that way, get more tone out of the drum? Instead of pounding on the drum, drawing, bringing, coaxing the sound out of the drum. Stinging the drum. Using less energy. It's a mental process of refining one's conceptual approach to expression through the drum set, 24 hours a day, 365 days a year.

GRUBER: I am wondering if the combination of two things, the drum and bugle corps and your time in the army, helped you learn how to conserve energy and prepare physically as a musician.

COBHAM: Army, yes. It was learning how to respond to the directions of my supervisors, my Non-Commissioned Officers. Do something? I did it. When I came in to the military, I was one step ahead of everybody. I came with that discipline. So, they listened to me a lot. That probably ended up saving my life, otherwise I would have gone to Vietnam. I was in the United States Army band. Was there from 1964, out in 1968.

GRUBER: How good a drummer were you when you left the army?

COBHAM: I was still pretty rough. My problem was the same positive element, all the discipline, now I had a problem just loosening up. I had help from Roy Haynes, one of my sponsors to get in to high school. We had jam sessions. This is a man at least 25 percent shorter and when he played on my drum set, I thought I had power, I had none. He knew how to attack the drums, bring out sound in drums. And you knew it was Roy when he was playing.

GRUBER: How did you meet him?

COBHAM: His nephew Artie Simmons played trombone, and was a leader of the first band that I ever joined, the Jazz Samaritans. We all lived in St. Albans, Queens, south Jamaica. Myself, George Cables, great jazz pianist, still lives in the same house out in Laurelton. Artie is still there as well, I believe.

We were inspired by what he (Haynes) was doing. He had a way, in his body language, to do some wonderful things, the way he challenged himself. He was a role model for us and still is to this day in his nineties.

GRUBER: OK, you complete your army stint, what happens then?

COBHAM: I got out of the military, already married, like an idiot, that is another part of the black social environment that I lived all my life. Living on love does not work. We wanted to do better, bringing up children, but we didn't know how, only knew we wanted to. I couldn't work, couldn't get a job, my wife had no idea where we went from there, I was just supposed to take care of everything. Her parents were also like that; we were just reliving that nightmare from the generation before us. I ended up starting to figure things out. but it had a very high cost. I made a lot of mistakes. I did silly things without thinking them through. The two innocent children I had with her, not their fault. I continued to make the same mistakes, learning, until finally on my fourth time around, I found the person who is with me now. That was a very heavy price to pay. All of the lessons are with me, how to work with people, why we go through what we go through.

GRUBER: In her head, was she marrying a musician, a potential star?

COBHAM: She was trying to get out of a problem that we both faced. Her parents and grandparents were separated, she had two brothers just getting by, she wanted to be an actress, she wanted the better things in life for herself. But we were too young to understand, we never really got it, there was no one there to tell us, the black woman in a family hating the black man because he wasn't there for her. Her father was a merchant marine, always on a ship, never met the man but that's the only way he could make a living. It was never enough. Then I had my family. At that time, my mom was the only one taking care of me and my brother. I had to be like a father to my brother. We had no idea how to help each other.

I'm The Baby: A Conversation with Wayne Cobham

Wayne Cobham is an accomplished trumpet player and Bill's younger brother. We met at a Billy Cobham Band performance at B.B. King's in New York. I asked him what happened in the Cobham home that inspired both brothers to develop a passion for music.

WAYNE COBHAM: It came from our parents. We got a chance to listen to a lot of music. My dad's family was poor and only one child was able to learn music, so his brother Edwin took piano lessons; but Dad would listen from the doorway, then try to replicate what he was hearing. He became a really good piano player; couldn't read charts, but played by ear. Mom was a good singer albeit not a professional, she was a church singer in choir, between an alto and a soprano. There was a need to find something for us kids to do and for Bill it became the Boy Scouts or Cub Scouts. First chance of playing an instrument was the Cub Scouts marching band. In Brooklyn, I had a first cousin Patrick, a lifetime army sergeant, and he came to our Jamaica house in his jeep, took Bill and I out to the local candy store. In the back of the jeep was a bugle. Bill picked it up and tried to make a sound but couldn't. I was able to blow a few notes and then I knew what my instrument was (*laughs*). I idolized my Dad and my brother, big shoes to fill. Dad was a strict disciplinarian to say the least and so when I tried to take lessons from Dad, such as fingerings on the piano, if I didn't hold my hands just right, I was scolded. Similarly, Bill started to progress and become prominent in drum and bugle corps; he became a star on the tenor drum, St. Catherine's Queensmen, Catholic Church out in Queens.

Bill always had tenacity and he practiced incessantly, on books, on beds, on anything he needed to gain that speed, dexterity. It was a rudiments game, 30-40 drummers and you had to play those selections exactly right. The judges would come and look down the drum line to see that the sticks were coming up and down the same way. That was in the junior corps. When he got older, he was in the senior corps, the *Long Island Sunrisers*, hotshot kid from Queens, won all these awards; he had to babysit me, so I would tag along. Bill comes in to the senior corps rehearsal and the guy says, 'I hear you can play, can you do this,' smoking a cigarette and doing a roll real fast with his right hand. Bill tried it, not quite as fast, and the guy says, you can get to the front of the line when you can do this. Bill says, OK, and came home and got *crazy* practicing, sometimes on a pillow, a rubber pad, and played all these rudiments so he could have a touch or a technique and be really good at it. Couple of months' time, they were auditioning front-line players. And Bill did it with both hands and backsticked it, and blew the guy away.

The neighborhood's outer surroundings weren't great, race relations, street violence, gangs. Mom and Dad thought, let's keep these kids out of that. I played with the *Sunrisers* as well. Got us out of the neighborhood, we got to play for championships in Pennsylvania, Connecticut, all around the country, learned how to play music, learned comradery. You had to be good, object was 21-51-101-200-piece band, you had to be as perfect as you could.

I'm the baby. I had big shoes to fill. As a jazz player, later on as a rock player, Cobham became a household name in the music industry. As a younger brother trying to establish myself as a horn player, many times I didn't have a chance to make a mistake, judged against my brother's prowess. A lot of time, early in my life, I would go to a jam with my horn, I would kick some ass or get my ass kicked.

GRUBER: Was your father supportive of your musical development?

WAYNE COBHAM: Mom raised us. Dad...back in the day, the Temptations had a great song, *Papa Was a Rolling Stone*. We didn't have Dad in the house all the time. However, as kids, when me and Billy were playing and got in trouble, "You boys better stop or I'm going to call your father." And when she made that phone call, Dad pulled up and we got disciplined. From time to time, Dad would take us to a baseball game or go for a ride in his car. That was our normal.

GRUBER: Did you ever go to a gig with your dad?

WAYNE COBHAM: Went to some of Billy's and he came to a couple of mine. Had a couple of chances to play with Dad. He always had a piano in the house in Virginia Beach. We would kick around and play some stuff. There is a video of the family playing a gig.

Dad had to come over to the United States and get a job, work that job, put money in the bank making $15 a week until he amassed enough capital to go to Immigration and bring the family over.

GRUBER: To what degree did your Panamanian and Caribbean heritage affect your musical identity?

WAYNE COBHAM: Latin music is what we heard a lot of in the household. If the grownups were having a party, that's what they would play. My mother's side, my grandparents were from Barbados, my father's side had roots from Haiti and beyond.

GRUBER: Why do you think Mahavishnu Orchestra caught fire in the way that it did? You had a close up look at what was happening in the culture and in the music business.

WAYNE COBHAM: Mahavishnu in the formative stages, it was all new. No one was doing that. *Take Five* was the only song in the market in a strange meter. When it came to an electric rock band, whose instrumentation was interesting - violin, fantastic guitar playing, Jan - crazy what they came up with, the tempos and melodies not heard before. No one was playing in a 7 or 9 or 14. All of the players were phenomenal. A lot of the stuff wasn't written down, it started out with maybe a groove (*Wayne scats a melody*), "What can I contribute to that?"

GRUBER: What was it that you saw in Bill at a young age that informed his music and his style?

WAYNE COBHAM: You had to learn the rudiments. A great foundation, and a proficiency to play them quickly with precision. Always pushing the envelope to do that one thing. I still get a kick after all these years, when he is playing a solo, I wonder if the crowd really knows how fucking hard that is, how that was ridiculously hard to pull off.

GRUBER: What kind of a big brother was he to you?

WAYNE COBHAM: A great supportive brother to me. It was tough love there too as well, he was always trying to push me to be better. A lot of musicians in that neighborhood, Marcus Miller grew up there, Donald Blackman, we didn't have games, we had bands. Everybody had a band. Basement of a friend's house, you played and played. So, if I knew the Brian Gruber band was going to be playing on Bedell Street and 130th Avenue next Saturday, great, I would put my band on the opposite corner, and there was a crowd down the block, and whoever could keep the crowd was the baddest band. J.T. Lewis was around, so many grew up in that tight little neighborhood of ours, you get your stripes by being known as someone who could play well. I was always trying to get to that point where I was accepted by my big brother. When I started doing some things, John Scofield, Kenny Kirkland, some of Bill's contemporaries started saying, "You got a brother who plays trumpet? He's *bad*." We played some things together. In Nice, France at MIDEM. That's the ultimate for me, being able to play with my brother, always a thrill for me. I learned a lot about musicianship, timeliness, professionalism from my brother.

Here's one story. Bill had a gig with the Jazz Samaritans. Didn't have a car to get to the gig. But he had a bicycle. He had a bass drum case, put a tom inside the bass drum, snare inside the tom and his hardware bag over his shoulder. The gig was four to five miles away and he got halfway there and fell off the bike. We all ran over, he ripped his suit. We told him we would get him home and get him cleaned up or take him to the hospital. He said, "No, I gotta get to the gig." So, he went and played his ass off. I watched him take his drums on the bus, he was insane. He was making his mark.

There's a record by James Brown. *King Heroin*. When you look at the credits, my brother played drums. I called him up and said, you never told me you played with James Brown. He said, yeah, he did.

Tuesday Night Backstage, Pre-Show

Guy and Bill review the first night's performance. There were moments, eight bars here, a couple of places there, where there was "just too much." On *Red Baron*, a horn player threw one of the solos to Carl Orr. Likely undetectable to the audience, but an example of real-time onstage communication and collaboration; Guy promises to "make it a bit more comfortable." He asks Bill what else they might adjust for tonight.

COBHAM: Great. I miss the trumpet in some parts. We have to drop it in later, to get it out more. When we go to recording, not now.

BARKER: When the trumpets are really going for it, everybody is going for it as well. It will be *fine*. (*Guy draws a storyteller's pause before elaborating*). There is a famous restaurant critic over here. He's on the TV a lot and he hosted a concert I did last year. He said, "Guy, we are going to have dinner. It's very simple. You come along, we sit. I buy you dinner and I don't listen to any of your opinions." He says, "The thing is, they will come up and they will say, 'How is everything?' Don't go, 'It's amazing.' You must only say, 'It's *fine*.' Then I can do my job." That was the rule. Next day I sent him a text, "Thanks so much for last night. It was *fine*." That's the thing. One of the worst things you can say to another musician is, "It was really *nice*."

Bill digs into a big helping of ice cream, adding, "It's a lot better than, 'Some of the things you did were OK.'" I ask Guy to tell me more about the horn players.

BARKER: Nigel Hitchcock, the first time I heard about him, people would say, (*lowers voice to a whisper*) there's this guy, this young kid, and he was playing with the national youth jazz orchestra, he was about 12 or 13 - I said, *"Really!?"* - and in that band, they had a big thick book of music. I used to play in that band when I was a teenager. It was like old school, all the charts were numbered, "Get out number 174," and they would draw on all these things, a big repertoire. Nigel was playing lead alto, and they were doing this gig outdoors and the wind was blowing, and it kept blowing the music off. So, in the end, he got so fed up with it, he took the music off the stand and put it on the floor under his chair and proceeded to play the whole gig off by heart. And then there was a saxophone quartet called *Itchy Fingers*, run by a guy called Mike Mower who is a very interesting composer, wrote great music with a dose of humor. And they were doing a tour and one of the saxophone players had broken his finger, swimming, and Nigel got the call and he got on the plane and they gave him this incredibly complex music. He sat down and sight-read it and, by the third gig, he left the music in the hotel room and did the whole thing by heart. It's freaky but amazing to have him in the middle of the section. Everybody has so much respect for him, but he is such a nice guy. He actually played on my very first album, he was about 16/17-years-old, and he wrote a couple of tunes and he was amazing.

I express interest in the order of the chairs.

BARKER: In the saxophones, you generally get first alto, second alto, first tenor, second tenor, baritone, that's the standard lineup. He is like your, the leader of the section is the first alto. Johnny Hodges (*Duke Ellington big band*) was the first alto, every band has its famous lead alto. And then of course, in the trumpet section, you always have to have a really strong lead trumpet, and this guy Nathan Bray plays lead for me all the time. But when I realized what it entails to translate Billy's music into big band music, and the strengths you need to have for it, I said I am going to sit on the end and I will give the other chairs to three amazing lead players. And then the trombone players, you've got Mark Frost who, for my money, is the best bass trombone player I have ever heard in my life.

GRUBER: He is at the far end, almost off stage. He didn't do any solos.

BARKER: No. He does improvise but he's not really an improviser like the other guys. He's incredible…he goes over to the States every year and performs with all the brass sections of the New York Phil and the Boston Symphony and they love him. Wycliffe Gordon, the trombone player who plays with Wynton, is a fan of Mark's.

GRUBER: I am not sure I have ever heard multiple trombonists soloing and blowing the doors off like they did last night.

BARKER: You've got Alistair White, who is a gritty, powerful bluesy-type player. I just love his playing. And Barnaby has phenomenal technique. He's got another thing going on.

Bill walks back in, declaring, "Hello everybody." Guy says we can carry on later but I ask, quickly, "From last night to tonight, how do you make an adjustment?"

BARKER: I might speak to Bill about incorporating the one tune we missed last night which means substituting. I think the thing to do is now stick with it, watch it get more and more solid. *(To Bill)* How were the kids, I hear it was fantastic.

COBHAM: Noisy but good, but they made sense.

GRUBER: They loved it and you looked like you were having a great time.

COBHAM: I was at the school eleven-thirty to one o'clock, then they had to come here one-thirty for set up. I didn't know exactly what the program was. I didn't know they were rehearsing to play here with me. I thought we did that at the school. I thought OK, fine, now what are we going to do? I ended up playing with them for 100 parents and kids that came from the surrounding area. That was amazing. But they had it down. They were serious about what they were doing at too young an age.

BARKER: That's wonderful.

Bill asks Guy if he got some rest.

BARKER: Yes, I got some rest. I saw my mother briefly. She was on her way to meet my aunt. My mum is going to be 90 in October.

COBHAM: Need a band? *(Laughter)*

BARKER: She is amazing. Then I came back and I did some more work. I am writing a cello concerto, so got a few more bars, a "few," maybe four or five.

COBHAM: I have a question for you. It makes me chuckle when we do it.

(Bill sings the notes of a specific part of a tune, immediately recognized by Guy, who joins in.) My original is, *(sings a slightly different riff clapping his hands)*, Light at The End of the Tunnel, and when I heard it, it was like, *bababa (clap) bababa*. Which one is it?

BARKER: In the version you sent me? The thing is, the first half is a direct transcription of the original recording. The second half is the file you sent me in 7/8 and 3/8.

COBHAM: Now I have to check. Did you bring the scores?

BARKER: In the end, I used my scores, it was too small for me to read, I used the big scores. *(Changing the subject after a pause.)* I figured that first set worked so well, I was wondering whether we could play *Two for Juan* in the second half and replace it with something, like maybe…

COBHAM: What about *Sal Si Puedes* as an opening tune for the second half…

BARKER: It's such a stamina buster.

COBHAM: Well, that's a good reason why not to do it *(laughs)*. It's a ball buster. But it's something to achieve.

BARKER: Could we do *2 for 1* instead of *Sal Si Puedes*? Some of the things work so well, I am already getting to the stage where 'I don't want to leave *that* out, or *that*.' That's why in that first set, *Obliquely* and then the medley, it's just perfect.

COBHAM: It should stay that way then. *(They debate the respective benefits of moving Cap Breton, which would expand the length of the set.)*

BARKER: A couple of guys were saying how much they liked *Two for Juan* and they missed it.

COBHAM: No problem then. It's a nice release. But remember also, in the second part, *Eggshells* can't go.

BARKER: No, no and *Le Lis* can't go. The only things I would ever…What do we start with? Do *Two for Juan*, then the medley, then *Le Lis*.

COBHAM: The wheelhouse we haven't explored is playing straight-ahead, and that's the only place that we can do it.

BARKER: Why don't we do *Two for Juan*, then the medley then *Le Lis*, then *Sal Si Puedes*, then see how that feels and maybe put *Cap Breton* back in tomorrow. I like the fact that it's all going on, and then suddenly it goes into that, and goes up slightly for the trombones…

COBHAM: In essence, what I am seeking to do is, keep this in tempo, and then cut it in half and then in half again, so when it comes back, we are still where we were. If I get it right. Did you eat?

GRUBER: (To Guy) Do you have a point at which you don't like to eat before the show? Half hour before?

BARKER: Yeah, 20 minutes. Tomorrow I'm going to go to yoga.

GRUBER: Bill, when you watch video of yourself from 40-some years ago, is there anything you could do with drums that you could not do now?

COBHAM: Honestly? Well. I could do everything I did then now. (But with) selectivity, logic, *'what the fuck did I want to do that for.'* And it works. Do all those notes really need to be there? Do I need to be flailing? Or can I just play (*thump!*) and it all works.

GRUBER: Was that part of that your stage persona?

COBHAM: That was enthusiasm. That was playing with people who I wanted to play with. That was my only defense mechanism. Say in the Cobham Duke Band. I knew that I was working with a bunch of thugs. I wasn't sure about George, it was the people who represented him, but the buck stops with the artist. Same with Mahavishnu. Once we got on the bandstand, we were a team. We were solid. We were all about the objective of playing the music as best we possibly could as a unit. We could feed off of each other, and move forward together. Then everything can fall apart or moved to another dimension offstage. Who is better than whom? Who is the alpha? It was not funny for me. The only way I felt I could deal with it was to play my ass off.

GRUBER: In any corporate environment, or group of humans, you have back-biting, greed, miscommunication, malicious intention, but is there something unique about the structure, the pressure, the dynamic of the music industry, about the injection of creative people into a unique business process that makes it extreme?

COBHAM: Yes. It continues to morph as rules change. Brown-nosing. It's all about knowing the right person to get what you want for yourself first and then whomever you may represent. That is a job unto itself, a cancer unto itself. That's a lot of energy to get to the point where you are controlling an environment.

GRUBER: Do you enjoy being on the road performing?

COBHAM: I don't mind being on the road. I don't enjoy it, I tolerate it. As Jan Hammer says, I wish I could dematerialize and show up on the concert stage and play and go back home the same way. That is why he stopped performing. It's not about like or dislike, it's about self-respect. Sustain yourself physically in a healthy way. Be in the best possible mental and physical condition you can be; chances are it will be a really good show. And someone in the audience will hear that and want you to do something else, because you took care of yourself.

> *I am liking it less not because of the touring itself but the travel is more and more difficult (Bill applauds). The airports are a particularly terrible thing, the airlines don't allow the bass inside the cabin, or in the luggage. They always bring the wrong size van to pick up the gear. It is just more and more difficult to get from Point A to Point C, which is the stage. Point B is you got to get to the hotel, you got to check in, you gotta find the luggage, it's always late. It's these events. Not to go and play in a different location, I like that, man. It's like a free acoustic school for me. How does this hall work? How does this strange bass work? But the process of getting to have the experience is what is so wearing and so damning.*
>
> *- Ron Carter* [4]

GRUBER: What's your advice to young musicians going on the road?

COBHAM: Have patience, this will take a while. Don't make your move

---

[4] From Brian Gruber's backstage interview at the Blue Note in New York on January 9, 2013, with Ron Carter, Billy Cobham and Donald Harrison Junior. youtu.be/CqEKo2zX0Rw

too fast. Observe what is going on. Come fully armed with knowledge. They want to be a star, and they haven't left the house yet.

GRUBER: Is there a uniquely Billy Cobham style of drumming?

COBHAM: Yeah, I think so. I am not afraid to say that. Because nobody is playing like me. What happens is this. First and foremost, it starts with the drum set. No one sets up their drums like me. That's number one. The next is where do I start my patterns from. No one does that like me. If I had a drum fill, I wouldn't necessarily play from the left to the right. All my patterns start from the center and go circularly in both directions at once, so I can do a lot of different things based on the fact that I studied to be ambidextrous when I played the drums. I'm unconventional in that respect. I took different-size drums in different positions so I could play that drum in what I felt was the most logical place for me to have it in relation to the other instruments in my performance environment. So, I have this clover leaf of sounds that I always deal with. The snare drum, a rack-tom on my left, a ride-cymbal over the rack-tom, and the hi-hat. That's really my drum set. With the bass drum, I've got a five-piece kit right there. All the other accoutrements are extra. They can be taken away. I can still play effectively.

Then there is the question of tuning. Most drummers don't tune. They are rhythmatists. They play rhythms. Some play them extremely well and consistently which means that their tempos are good, but the application of rhythm is not playing musically. What I am seeking to do is play patterns that have tones. Just as if I was playing a marimba (*ba-da-da-ba*). Or choosing certain tones in certain pieces of music that keep the whole harmonic structure connected. Multi-tasking, playing rhythmically but melodically as well on top. Yeah, no one is doing that.

The star treatment is so: eight lugs on a drum. I think I have one six lug drum. It hails from the 1920s. You tighten one and you go across the drum, you form a star. There are two heads on my drum sets. One head is for tuning to bring pitch correctly, the other head is to determine the character of the sound. Thirty to thirty-five percent of the sound, the tonal character of the drum, is dependent on how that bottom head is tensioned to promote the sound when you put stick to head.

GRUBER: You seem to spend a lot of time with drum companies to get the sound that you want. Why is that important to you?

COBHAM: It's important to have a major manufacturer who builds your equipment to suit you. As an artist, I have supplies on demand. It's important to have a drum set in different regions, close to where you normally play, so you don't have to ship long distances. The chance of loss or damage in transit is diminished greatly.

I started with Tama drums, 1977, I think, to 1987. They decided to change their policy so I decided to not continue with them. Then, Mapex out of Taiwan, stayed with them for 10 years. Then, made an offer to Yamaha, all I wanted to do was to have them put the drums in place. Worked with Yamaha till 2013, when Tama asked me to rejoin their company. They had a new line. They make incredibly good stuff. Yamaha is a Bentley. You go to Tama and you got a Rolls. I got four sets of bubinga, two in Europe and two in the United States.

GRUBER: I remember our drive to the Craviotto studio south of Santa Cruz.

COBHAM: The head guy passed away. He was a craftsman, he made things look beautiful. Then you have to find a way to make them sound beautiful. The drums are not for everybody, made for a very small group of people. He was an artisan. In the stratosphere for cost. A Craviotto snare drum costs $2,400. Someone could buy five kits for that.

GRUBER: Is there something unique about the way you experiment with gear or companies?

COBHAM: That's important. The added value for me is I don't want an assembly line drum. If I am going to represent a company it is has to be exactly what I need to play on. So, we got into the technical aspects. It starts with a shell that gives me a good vibrative tone, then the depth of the shell, between a 5.5 snare and a 7 is where I wanted to be. Then it is the heads. All the lugs had to be uniformly placed and a certain material. The weight of the metal affects the vibration of the head. Heads used top and bottom. When you hit the batter head, the bottom goes *wwwwooowwooo* and holds the tone. How the drums hold up traveling and storage-wise. No anvil cases anymore with 2.5 tons of gear to go to LaGuardia curbside and give a guy $20 to put on a DC-9. How the things are set up, bring a five-kilo head set to change everything. Playing on something set specifically for me. Manufacturers go by the numbers and it's up to the artist to see what works in terms of how they present their musical personality through the drum set.

GRUBER: Tell me about your early experiments with electronic drumming.

COBHAM: 1968. Hollywood Miazzi, out of Milano, distributed by Carl Fisher Music out of New York. Me and Tony Williams and DeJohnette and I think Max (Roach) were each given a set to try on the road. I received them in a box, a personal stage with wheels. All you had to do was take the cymbals off when travelling with the kit. Put a square hat box on top and latch it down in four places. That went on a plane as luggage. The cymbals were real but sounded like (*tch-tch*). That didn't work so well. Then we went to Tama and they made electric drums, beginning of '80's and the disco thing, and that was awful. After Tama, I didn't play electronic drums again until Yamaha. They finally had it all together. I found I was creating sequences and there were patches, other exotic sounds like gongs that you couldn't take on the road anymore for logistical reasons. So, you had a gong sample, cowbells, different sounds and tones and pitches. All works. You can capture sounds, create a melody sequence and capture and play along. It helped in the show as a great tool and added dimension.

GRUBER: What do you consider your most important collaborations? Do you prefer running the show yourself?

COBHAM: I love to play with people. Where they respect what I do and, musically speaking, offer me something that I can take from them and work with.

My first major collaboration that I really enjoyed was working with Billy Taylor and with Chris White, who also played bass with Dizzy and Nina Simone. Why? Because I learned a lot of jazz standards working at the Hickory House, the last jazz club on 52nd Street. It had this trio behind the bar. We had to start at 8, didn't finish until 2. Forty-five minutes, 15-minute break, six shows a night. 1967. I was moonlighting, being in the Military Ocean Terminal Band, the 178th, at just below the Verrazano Bridge in Brooklyn. Did that for six months toward the end of my stint in the army, learned a lot. Eddie Thompson, blind pianist from England, a lexicon of music, Jaki Byard, great alto saxophonist out of Boston, (was also a) great pianist when Mingus was there. They would just rattle off tunes. What I was left with was an amazing ability to retain songs in my head. Can't even remember the names but learned them, played them over and over again.

Fast forward to the beginning of the millennium, I get a mandate to play four concerts if I can put together a trio with Ron Carter and Kenny Barron, and the next thing you know we are talking about these tunes. We meet in Naples, Kenny from Montevideo, Ron from New York. We play the following day, no rehearsals, nothing. We did a sound check and shared only song titles and Kenny starts to play. I can't do that with too many people.

GRUBER: You generally play your own compositions in your shows. Do you ever play standards just because it would be fun?

COBHAM: I always play standards because it's fun, but it is part of my heritage, music that was created by masters of the past still in the minds of masters of the present. Once you learn these tunes. it's like studying Brahms or Beethoven; what were these guys or women actually thinking? Normally it is highly subjective, you are writing based on something you have experienced in life offstage. What helps me with the Brubeck project, most of these tunes I know. Most of the people in the band can't even pronounce the names, much less what it may mean. And those are the professionals. It's kind of beautiful to be able to walk in and be comfortable enough to do this.

GRUBER: If you had one concert to do jazz standards at the club of your choice, what would you include?

COBHAM: Send me an email. I'll give you the answers.

I did. And he did.

A Portrait of Jenny (Claude Debussy/D. Tiomkin)
Sweet Lorraine (Cliff Burrell)
So What (Miles Davis)
Green Dolphin Street (Bronislaw Kaper)
St. Thomas (Sonny Rollins)

The Night Has a Thousand Eyes (Ben Weismann)
Watermelon Man (Herbie Hancock)
But Beautiful (Jimmy Van Heusen)
Four (Miles Davis)
My Funny Valentine (Richard Rogers)
Blue in Green (Miles Davis/ Bill Evans)
Fables of Faubus (Mingus)
Moanin' (Bobby Timmons)
Round Midnight (Thelonious Monk)
I Thought About You (Jimmy Van Heusen)

GRUBER: How did you meet Billy Taylor, and what it was like to play with him so many hours each night?

COBHAM: How did we meet? (*Long pause.*) I know, I know. There used to be something called Jazzmobile, Billy was an advocate. He had a radio program for a long time, *WLIB-AM*. He would promote jazz and play it and speak very eloquently. Very important, especially in those days; black people were presented to the general public as being second-class citizens, not having the ability to speak English properly in general. That was all negative marketing. Then, along comes this guy, with music that was well-received by all society, as a DJ with a small listening-audience radius, and he is speaking quite eloquently about music and its foundations and people who influence him. He would present great stuff. When I worked with George Cables, Jazz Samaritans, we met Mr. Taylor many times. We looked up to this person, he knew everyone in the black community from Jackie Robinson, whoever.

We used to play in contests and if you won, you got a chance to play Sunday matinees at the top of the Village Gate, Art D'Lugoff's place, and a new place called Your Father's Moustache. That eventually changed to the Bottom Line, on the NYU campus. Alan Pepper ran the Bottom Line with a guy named Stan Snadowski. Alan was the frontman, worked closely with Billy Taylor. We won a couple of contests.

I made the penultimate mistake of not being able to get to a gig because of the army switching commitments at the last minute. So, either go AWOL and go to jail, or go to the gig. I never played with Billy again until just before he died a few years ago.

GRUBER: Was your work with (keyboardist) George Duke an important musical period for you?

COBHAM: I remember our musical ideas worked very well together. I brought John Scofield (guitar) into the concept, Alphonso Johnson was the last bass player involved. We had good chemistry musically. It wasn't to go very far. We lacked one very important element, management. George had a manager who was quite dominant, management by intimidation, Zappa band manager Herb Cohen. Didn't leave things to chance. He controlled the purse strings, So, even though my name was at the top of our presentation marquee, I was not in a position to make changes. I could accept it for a while because I didn't think it would be permanent. Was I exploited? I was. Herb Cohen and George Duke became a classic situation where you had a goon as management, some kind of gangster, *"You will never work in this club again."* George worked on my *Crosswinds* album, and four or five of my records.

Bill has positive memories of Cohen as well, "amazing conversations with Herb over wonderful meals."

COBHAM: There is a great story where a call comes in to Ted Turner's office looking for a Warner Brothers act for a Christmas concert with Pope John Paul XXIII. Dylan had been there the year before. They refer them to Montreux to Claude Nobs who is Senior Vice President of Entertainment for Warner Brothers Europe. Claude referred them to California to Quincy Jones, Qwest Records. His secretary said maybe you should talk to Herb Cohen, who promised to get back to him. He says, we don't have anybody available. What would it take, asks the Bishop? Cohen says, it would take an audience with the Pope. He gets George to go, his wife is Filipina, a devout Catholic. Herb never likes to wear a suit and tie, but wears one.

He wants to do right by his employees so he goes to George, puts his hands in his pockets, and takes out both hands full of Trojan condoms. George's eyes fall out. Herb wants the Pope to bless them for his secretaries and staff. George says I will disown you. Pope John was the bishop of Williamsburg, Brooklyn. They have the audience, everyone stands in line, goes by rather quickly. The Pope is Polish, gets to George, then Herb, who says, "Sistine Chapel, nice place you got here." Herb mistakenly drops a condom on the floor and quickly picks it up.

Wonderful conversations with Herb. That same Doctor Jekyll becomes Mister Hyde when it comes to the music business. You never knew what was going to happen with him. That says a lot to me about the music business in general.

GRUBER: Most memorable collaboration?

COBHAM: Horace Silver. Ten months. I had a ball. The problem was there wasn't any money. I ended up bringing two innocent individuals into the world before I was ready to have kids. I realized I didn't have a family life, always working, always on the road. All he could pay me was $250 a week and I had to pay hotel and food out of that. He gave me a gift, a suit that he got at a discount. That is all he could really afford to do. (Bandmates were) Randy Brecker, John B. Williams, Bennie Maupin. He was really correct about everything, a very good teacher. "Sorry, man, I don't have any more money, if you choose to leave I understand." The quality of his material was top-end, wonderful. Very sincere with me.

GRUBER: You mentioned being in the pit in Broadway shows like *Promises, Promises*.

COBHAM: I found as quickly as possible I was not cut out for that because I was adding more to the written parts than was needed to keep the show flowing. I didn't have the discipline or the experience in working Broadway shows. I was hungry. I wanted the job for a payday. A lot of the drummers that play in the pit are there for the rest of their lives or careers. They are doing the same thing over and over again until they could do it as they were reading the newspaper. I think I did *1776* for a split second. I thought, this was not me, and went back to the studio scene.

GRUBER: Then there was Dreams.

COBHAM: 1969 until Mahavishnu 1971. Randy and Michael Brecker, Barry Rogers on trombone. John Abercrombie was brought in by the Brecker brothers, they were friends. Don Grolnick on keyboards, used to play with James Taylor. Will Lee on bass, just before I left, young kid from

Miami. Became the bass player on the Letterman show, (with) David Sanborn and has accomplished so much in the music scene.

GRUBER: What did you seek to accomplish with Dreams?

COBHAM: Play as a band. We were gifted. I was invited to join the band by Barry Rogers, trombone player, who had a strong resume in the Latin field. I was 25. Horn section ran that band. And Randy and Michael were the best and most accomplished horn players on the New York City scene at the time. Eddie Vernon, lead singer. Chuck Rainey (bass) came and left. We talked about bringing in Tony Levin. I was against it because I thought he played too many notes back then.

GRUBER: You had some interesting rehearsal experiences. Hendrix on one floor, Janis Joplin on another. Was that Electric Lady studio?

COBHAM: That was Baggy's rehearsal studio, rehearsing with Dreams, 1969. Jimi was putting together Band of Gypsies with Buddy Miles on drums and Billy Cox on bass. We were on the top, the most dangerous floor. It was a gutted factory, five or six stories. People could rent the place and play as long as they wanted, and that would become home. Joplin was below, Big Brother and the Holding Company, the music would just reverberate through the floors. We were preparing to go on tour.

Cobham and Brecker

Randy Brecker is a near-constant presence throughout Billy Cobham's musical career, often teamed with brother Michael. From Horace Silver and Dreams to the *Spectrum* tour, then four decades of intersecting recordings, performances and friendships.

COBHAM: What makes Randy Brecker stand out as one of the greatest living trumpet players, he made everything sound so logical. He just played the right notes at the right time. Randy was always working. What's amazing is he has a gift to express himself through his instrument as if he is holding a really good conversation with the listener through his horn. These days, he is a complete throwback to the way most trumpet and wind players used to play back in the day. He has all of these experiences working with Clark

Terry and all these cats from back then. We were on the road together in 1968 with Horace Silver. He had this way as a solo player.

I called Randy at his Hamptons home before he headed out for a show in Japan to talk about his decades-long series of collaborations with Bill.

RANDY BRECKER: We met in 1967. I joined the Horace Silver quintet after leaving Blood Sweat & Tears because I wanted to play jazz. And Billy was the drummer.

GRUBER: How long did you play with him and Horace?

BRECKER: The band stayed together for a year and a half. Sometime in 1969, Horace broke up the band. We came back to New York without a gig; Horace gave us two weeks notice. In the interim, my brother had moved to New York a couple of months earlier and met a trombone player named Barry Rogers. Who in turn had met two singer/ songwriters, Jeff Kent and Doug Lubahn, and they were looking for a trumpet player and a drummer. They had a band they were starting called Dreams. So we suggested ourselves. And the band was born. With the six of us.

Also when we got back, we worked with a guy Edwin Birdsong who went on to produce Roy Ayers, became a very successful producer, a kind of a James Brown influence. We played together with Dreams for a couple years, two albums, then John McLaughlin started Mahavishnu Orchestra so Billy left for a couple of years. Mike and I went back to work with Horace Silver ...

Billy did his first solo record *Spectrum* which became a big hit. He left Mahavishnu and included Mike and I in his new band. We stayed in that band around 1974 and 1975 after which time we started the Brecker Brothers. There was pretty much a seven-year period where I played with Billy constantly. We played on three or four albums over a couple of years. I had been writing some material, Mike and I left for Arista Records, we left on good terms, and I have been playing off and on with him every since. I got my first Grammy in a week I was playing with Bill at Ronnie Scott's. I forgot it was Grammy week and I was informed that I won in the middle of a set. We talk a couple of times a year and I come see him play when he is in New York.

GRUBER: What was your aspiration for the Dreams band? What did you hope it would achieve commercially and artistically?

BRECKER: We were hoping artistically it would be more on the jazz side of the jazz-rock continuum. Billy was the centerpiece of the band. No one plays like that. I was probably the only one who saw this development. From Horace's band where he played a normal jazz set and I watched incredulously as he gets interested in what some of the rock drummers were doing, two bass drums, more drums, and I saw him bulking up - he was always well-built - and slowly change his thinking. When we started Dreams, we were hoping we could take advantage of all the great things he could do on the drums. He just flabbergasted people because no one had played that way before. He literally created that style, of jazz-rock - later known as fusion - drumming by combining several sources. There is no other word than he flabbergasted people. And of course, it was a great musical undertaking; with my brother, the horn section was great. We hoped we would sell a lot of records. We tried for hits but I think we were too musically inclined, the experience was really a live thing that you had to see. It never coalesced as far as the records although they are great records. They didn't have the same kind of commercial appeal that Blood, Sweat & Tears and Chicago did. Eventually, it was time to call it a day and when Billy left, we auditioned close to 60 drummers. I'll never forget that. Everyone in town, even Steve Gadd who had just moved to New York. He was still a jazz drummer and hadn't quite figured out the Steve Gadd school of drumming, which he did figure out later. I eventually figured, it was time to let it fly, to let the thing go.

GRUBER: How meaningful is the word fusion to you? You were there at the beginning and participated in a number of those efforts. At the time, amidst all the experimentation, what did you make of the integration of jazz, rock, Latin, funk, and other forms?

BRECKER: It was just a very exciting time because we were communicating to a larger audience. I think all of us felt the golden age of jazz/ bebop/ the Blue Note years peaked, and we didn't want to repeat things that had been done. Guys like Freddie Hubbard or Tony Williams or Horace Silver, Herbie and Wayne, we didn't want to go in that direction, we didn't want to repeat things, we wanted to try to do something new. Pop music was coming into its own, some great things happening, we had all grown up in that element, and being in New York, being around the whole thing, being around Latin music, we wanted to try something different. And we were not alone in that regard. There were a lot of bands who were coming along with the same idea, Chick's band Return to Forever, Herbie, I saw that metamorphosis with his various groups, and of course McLaughlin and others of that ilk. So, we all kind of came up together with forward-thinking ideas.

I mention the first concert I attended, the triple-bill at the Fillmore East, the month that *Bitches Brew* was released.

BRECKER: Oh yeah, wow. I might add a lot of these bands revolved around the things that Miles was doing with *Bitches Brew* and a lot of the other groups grew out of that.

GRUBER: You had been around for some years before that release, playing with the likes of Larry Coryell. Did you believe that there were artists and forms of experimentation prior that deserved equal recognition?

BRECKER: It's funny you asked that. We were a little bit ahead of that. I'll tell you a funny story. It goes to show you where maybe Miles was influenced himself. Dreams became kind of the house band at the Village Gate, a large club on Bleeker Street, now closed for many years. That was one of the hippest if not the hippest place to play in New York. Miles would play there, in fact I saw him in a double bill with Charles Lloyd with his great band with Jack DeJohnette and Keith Jarrett. That was an amazing double bill. Miles would come down and never come and talk to us, but you always knew when he was there, everyone saying, "Miles is here," which spread around the audience like wildfire. You could see him sitting in the back. In the meantime, I had electrified my trumpet. We had John Abercrombie in the band who always played with a wah-wah pedal. One day he couldn't make rehearsal and his pedal was just sitting there and we had these devices called 'condors' which made bubbly sounds on the horn and I plugged the wah-wah into my trumpet and it sounded just great. I got a wah-wah myself and started using it, using guitar effects and Miles would always come down. Eventually he hired Billy for *Bitches Brew*. When I joined

Billy's band, there was a guy named Jim Rose, who was Miles' road manager, would come by the gig and say I was trying to sound like Miles with the wah-wah, and I explained to him the way things had developed. It became a running joke between me and Jim. He liked Billy so he would come to hear us a lot.

Years later when we were all at (Brecker brothers-owned jazz club) Seventh Avenue South, I found myself standing next to Miles. The club was really crowded. I never really met him so I stuck out my hand and said, "Hi, I'm Randy Brecker, I'm a big fan, I own the club and it's great to meet you," and his response was...nothing. He had his dark glasses on so it was just silence, he just kind of looked through me. I slunked away, went downstairs to the bar and started having a couple of martinis. About an hour later, I hear a little wisp of air in my left ear, "*I love my wah-wah, you love your wah-wah.*" And he split. It was the only thing he said to me (*laughter*). He was still a big influence, especially when it started, it was a little later that *Bitches Brew* got recorded but then his influence was undeniable when he put together that great electric band. I know it influenced Billy. It influenced all of us.

GRUBER: It fascinates me that Bill at 73 is not only touring a lot but almost every year producing new music. What is it for men like you and Bill that motivates you to continue to create and innovate when you can simply play other people's music or rely on things you might have done years ago?

BRECKER: It's a good question and I don't know if I can put myself on a level of Billy's output, which is really just incredible, but I think it has to do with, after you do something, it gets old pretty quickly. So, we are always trying, we just want to play something new, we can't rest on our laurels too long. Plus, this is what we do. We don't have many outside interests. You find that with a lot of great artists. I'm very close for instance with Paul Simon, and a tour manager that works with Paul and Bob Dylan. I asked him the same question, how come most guys are still killing themselves on tour? Not everybody has to do it. He said, "Look man, they don't know what else to do with themselves." Other than play, write music and tour, I don't have a lot of outside interests. Of course my famIly, I want to be home sometime, but that's what motivates us I think. We love to play. And for my money, I think Bill is, I swear to God, playing better than ever. I heard him in Brazil, maybe two, three years ago with Jeff Berlin and Scott

Henderson, it was a trio and man, he just played better than ever. Everything is just settled now. It's incredible.

GRUBER: When you watch him in YouTube videos from the '70s and '80s, to now, he really does have quite a physical presence.

BRECKER: And let me say one other thing. In the ensuing years, I wouldn't play with him regularly, more like a special guest thing. But every time I did, I noticed he always brought something new to the table. Not only new music, the way he played, it always fascinated me. Some kind of new drum that he invented or something I never heard before. That alone, throughout the years, is quite an accomplishment.

GRUBER: Do you have some favorite memories on or off-stage?

BRECKER: There are a lot of them. How do I narrow it down? I was just always completely knocked out playing with him. (*Laughs.*) I probably shouldn't say this. I remember he was so confident of his playing – as he should have been because I think he was the greatest drummer and still is – but when drum machines first came out, he tried to overdub the drum machine over his track. That didn't work too well. I remember the look on his face.

GRUBER: Where do you think he fits in the history of percussion? How would you sum up his cumulative contribution to the music world?

BRECKER: He always would mention Tony Williams and Jack. After that period it was just Billy as far as I am concerned. The guy who originated the whole thing was Bill. The fact that he has been playing so long and is still this great, places him at the forefront of jazz drumming, of composition. He has had the same kind of influence on drummers that Jaco had on bass players.

GRUBER: What are you doing these days?

BRECKER: I am still writing, touring, I manage to do a lot with my own band and collaborating with other people. I am leaving next week for Japan with an all-star band, with Steve Gadd, Lou Marini, old friends. This summer, I am co-leading a band with Mike Stern, with the great Lenny White on drums in Europe for two or three weeks. Will tour the U.S. with

Dennis Chambers, always recording with a lot of people, just came back fronting a big band in Kazakhstan doing a night of my music which was a thrill.

After the interview, Randy sends an email with one last story.

BRECKER: OK, one road story I meant to recount when you asked.

We were recording in London after a UK tour and/ or a gig at Ronnie's... think we were maybe recording one of my tunes...Whatever it was, it was a somewhat complicated piece, and I had a late flight booked back to NYC that same evening. It started getting close to when I needed to get out to the airport, so I expressed that sentiment to Billy... we had done a couple of takes of the tune already...so Billy says, "OK, we'll get you outta' here." And it was like when you turn the flame on your stove from medium to high...perfectly balanced...his whole body...he ratcheted it up a notch and the next thing I know we had the take, and I was in the cab to the airport. The surety of his, "OK we'll get you outta' here" statement combined with the precise way he musically upped the ante was unforgettable.

Back in the club, Bill asks about our interview schedule and I mention I have a call with Jan Hammer. We discuss meeting at 6:30pm tomorrow for our next conversation. Bill needs some rest after a non-stop day. Before we go, he shows off the lyrics to the *Billy Cobham* tune written and artfully presented in poster form by the Soho kids. "Wow," Guy is impressed. "How lovely."

Paul Price on Designing Cover Art

Tonight, at the Ronnie Scott's bar, I happen upon Paul Price, who redesigned Cobham album art as a college art project and, years later, found himself Bill's CD cover designer. Paul has seen countless shows over the years. As the concert ends, I ask him how this one was different.

PRICE: The show was great, amazing arrangements of the old classics with a few curve balls. What impresses me the most about these shows is the amount of work that goes into them; I'm guessing these were set lists just for *Ronnie Scott's*.

I ask Paul how he came to design many of Bill's album covers.

PRICE: The *Spectrum* story is a dream come true. At my first art college in '88-89, I was introduced to the Mahavishnu Orchestra by a hippie lecturer. A friend and I would travel down to London Tower Records and ask the jazz guy to recommend LP's. *Spectrum* was one of the first recommended. Along with the insane drumming came a rock guitarist and serious groove. For my final design exhibition, I made up a jazz label, and Billy Cobham's *Spectrum* was one of three CD covers I redesigned.

After leaving college and making a name for myself in design, I emailed Billy and was surprised to get a reply. I don't have the email, but it was mid-2000. They say don't meet your heroes, but he was funny, kind, creative, and passionate. We went for a meal at a place that only sold sausages in Soho, Billy will remember. I had a bag of CDs I wanted signed in case I never saw him again. I needn't have worried. I did seven or eight of his covers over the next 17 years, and two years ago I did the *Spectrum Live 40* cover, a fulfilment of a young designer's dream.

GRUBER: How do you collaborate with Bill on the cover art?

PRICE: The creative process is quite simple. Sometimes Billy knows exactly what he wants, but I have to inform him if the art is going to cost a lot to use. More importantly, I ask, "What's the style, we going fusion or jaaaaaaazz?"

I then do a load of ideas, very different. Hopefully, Billy will like one idea, then we tighten it up and move on. A surprising amount of work goes into it, but it's all worth it to work for a hero, that even after 17 years never lets me down with his music live, on CD or in the way he tells his tales. His passion for his art still surprises me. And that we hear that every time he plays. The latest Ronnie shows are a perfect example.

3 MILES, MAHAVISHNU, MONTREUX

Prior to coming to London for the Ronnie Scott's run, Bill worked with a 17-piece Swiss youth orchestra on a Dave Brubeck tribute, performing *Take Five, Blue Rondo a la Turk,* and *In Your Own Sweet Way,* among others. I'm curious what he was doing with the project.

COBHAM: I play the drums, mentor, and teach. We play the music together. Brubeck was an oddity in 1957-58. People didn't play in five in the United States, they couldn't even play in three. In the U.S., you either played in two or four for marches and swing and all that kind of stuff. Playing in two or four started to take hold again with smooth jazz, the 'birth of the cool.' Miles Davis, Gil Evans. When you listen to those recordings, they are laid back. 'Nothing bothers me.' The look of a person on a corner leaning on a lamp post outside of a club at 2 o'clock in the morning playing the 4th of 6th shows he has to play. Gerry Mulligan contributed to this on the West Coast, baritone saxophone, trumpet playing in the mid-range, Chet Baker, Stan Getz.

GRUBER: You played with Getz.

COBHAM: He stood in front of me and played at Montreux, 1977. In that band was Dexter Gordon, Hubert Laws, George Duke, Bob James, two keyboard players. Alphonso Johnson played bass. Eric Gale played guitar. Recorded as *Montreux Summit (considered by many one of the great jazz jam sessions of all time)*. Getz was one of the featured artists. Kind of an all-star thing (others in the jam included Woody Shaw, Steve Khan, Benny Golson). Scheduled as such. Don't recall playing with him again.

Bill calls up a recent email from Getz's widow Monica. She explains, "One of Stan's unfulfilled wishes, before he died, was to get a project released that he started in Israel." She goes on to explain that Stan "... always mentioned he would have liked to involve you in the project. If you ever are in the U.S., would you let me know? I have tried to locate you for some time, of course I remember you very well." Bill mentions seeing Getz at Rockefeller Plaza at the top of the RCA building, with an interesting quartet, "Chick Corea, a leprechaun of a drummer named Tony Williams, Stanley Clarke."

GRUBER: What is your calculus for evaluating a project like that?

COBHAM: I ask questions. I have to teach in Tel Aviv. I am just going to get up and go because it's Stan Getz? I don't think so. Someone will have to present music to me, then I'll listen and say, yes, this is something I would like to contribute to. Yes, Stan Getz, but who else is playing on the thing? Names don't determine the quality of the music.

GRUBER: The early *Getz/ Gilberto* album, his collaboration with Brazilian musicians, what role did that have in the early development of fusion?

COBHAM: It opened up another route. People interested in more than one or two directions. There are specialists, the jazz police, people who only play in a dark, dingy club in the cellar as if they are running away from the gestapo. Only (interested in) people who emulated Charlie Parker. There are other people who played more openly, the directions, the template and concept of jazz. What would it be like to play a little *boogaloo* inside this, *samba*, how about *tango*, Piazzolla? That's considered jazz now. It's like a centipede with a lot of legs.

GRUBER: When did fusion become a distinct genre in your view? As a teenager growing up in New York, and for many others, Mahavishnu is the first band that I recall presented as fusion, or jazz-rock.

COBHAM: Started in 1967 first and foremost. Why, because there was a 17, 18-year-old kid (Tony Williams) playing drums with Miles in 1964. Three years later, *E.S.P.* showed up. (Starts singing a melody *bee-boo-dee…*). And they went off in that direction. It all made sense to move ahead. 'Birth of the Cool' was boring after a while. As was its follower 'smooth jazz.' Like going from wide ties to thin ties to…With better sound on FM. That's where your dental music was coming from.

GRUBER: Dental music. Now there's a genre. Back to 1967. *Bitches Brew* was in studio two years after that, released in 1970, had the reputation of *the* breakthrough jazz fusion album. Was that because of record sales, notoriety and promotion? Was *E.S.P.* more of a musical breakthrough?

COBHAM: *E.S.P.* was more of a breakthrough but much more eclectic, and therefore didn't come anywhere close to selling like *Bitches Brew*. On the *E.S.P.* cover, you saw Frances Davis, Miles' wife, beautiful dancer, wonderful artist in her own right. *Bitches Brew* had this very dramatic cover on it. It carried a bigger story. Whatever was happening at that time, a ball of confusion in the U.S., politically and otherwise, that music represented a lot of things to people. The seed that started fusion was *ESP*.

> *The cover of* Bitches Brew *is set within a world of light and dark. A black and white woman intertwine their heads and fingers while an image of menacing clouds lies opposite a fierce tribal woman and a peaceful dark figure. Klarwein's contradictive themes depicted in the piece - anger and love, intimacy and loneliness, strength and weakness - work as a grand attempt to capture the vastness of humanity and the possibility for opposing characteristics in all of us.*
>
> *…For many, the sounds and images of* Bitches Brew *were intrinsically linked to the political climate, and specifically the racial climate of the early '70s. The cover's decidedly Afro-centric and psychedelic undertones reverberated within both the Black Power movement and the progressive counterculture of the early '70s…* [5]

GRUBER: When did you first meet Miles Davis?

COBHAM: I was working at the top of the Village Gate, with Phil Woods or Junior Mance.1969. Downstairs, Miles was working with Chick (Corea)

---

[5] Ritchie, Nora. "The Story Behind Mati Klarwein's Bitches Brew Album Art." *ReviveMusic.com*. December 16, 2010.

and Jack DeJohnette, Wayne (Shorter), Dave Holland, I believe. In between sets, Jack says, "Billy, I am going to leave Miles, would you be interested in taking my place?" I said, "Sure," and Jack says, "I'll have him call." Jack was straight up. I always felt, gee, it would great to be in a position to take the mantle from Tony and see what I could do with Miles for a little while.

Following day, my girlfriend is grumbling when I come in. I ask her, "What's the problem?" She says some idiot was trying to bust her chops about me doing something. I said, "OK. What?" She says, "I could not make out what he was saying, he kept whispering." Alarm bells start to go off. She said he was brazen and she got upset because she couldn't understand what he was saying. Miles whispered more than he talked, he had a problem with his vocal cords, so he didn't speak very loudly, though was forceful in what he had to say.

I say, "OK, what's his phone number?" I call and say, "Hey Miles, this is Billy Cobham." He says, "Rehearsal is at CBS at 10 o'clock." I walk in the following morning at nine; everybody was getting ready. Amazing. I had never seen so many piano players in a studio at the same time, and haven't since, especially *these* piano players. Larry Young on organ, Joe Zawinul, Keith Jarrett. All together in the same room and later Herbie shows up, and I went, wow, to be able to command that kind of respect is just *beyond beyond beyond*. People who wanted to be associated with him. It was in the music. And it sounded amazing. It showed how much people could work together, sometimes just by silently being supportive and waiting their turn to make their point if need be, or being supportive in a certain way, hearing something that could enhance what the other person was playing.

GRUBER: Did they come because they were commissioned to play on different tunes?

COBHAM: I don't know. They all seemed to play at the same time to me. They were there from the beginning until the end. Some people played on one thing or the other. I don't recall anyone saying to the other guy, "I am going to play *here* and *here*." That was the beauty of it. I wasn't the only drummer. Tony was there as well. These were called the *Bitches Brew* sessions. All kinds of people were there, in and out. It was amazing to be a fly on the wall and be honored just to be in their presence.

GRUBER: How long did you play with him?

COBHAM: 1983-4, I was in Japan with the Gil Evans big band and Miles. What I did with Miles was between 1969/'70, '71. Recordings, *Bitches Brew, Jack Johnson, Circle in the Round, Live/ Evil, On the Corner.*

GRUBER: Did you spend time with him outside of the studio?

COBHAM: No. He wanted me to join the band and I respectfully declined. I saw myself doing something else and I had to follow my dream.

GRUBER: That must have been a tough decision.

COBHAM: No, it wasn't.

Meeting McLaughlin: "Are you busy?"

GRUBER: Did you meet John McLaughlin through Miles?

COBHAM: No, I met him at Ronnie Scott's briefly in 1968, end of my tour with Horace Silver. He and Dave Holland left for New York to be with Tony right after that meeting. (In 1971) I was doing a soundtrack, the *Anderson Tapes,* James Bond-type, Sean Connery movie, took Grady Tate's place and John was one of the four guitarists on that session, Jim Hall, Eric Gale, Joe Beck. It was a Quincy Jones project, and for some reason, John wouldn't take directions from those guys. Quincy didn't like his attitude or something, I guess they fired him. It was not like he really cared. He said to me as he was leaving, "Are you busy, would you help me out, there are some things I would like you to hear." I said, OK, and he said, "Meet me at Baggy's." For about two weeks, it was just us, working together on tunes, just a duo, drums, and guitar.

GRUBER: Tell me about your personal connection with John.

COBHAM: It was about the music; I was intrigued by what he was playing. All like this odd meter thing, it was a weakness and I needed to focus on it. He helped me out a lot with that. Just by playing. No talk, just playing patterns. John would say, "I want to try this other thing" and he would play a line. He is an amazing person, when he gets his head wrapped around something, a narrow beam focus.

Next thing I know, (rock violinist) Jerry Goodman came, and we started to play with a bass player, Charlie Haden, made this record called *My Goal's Beyond* on Hendrix's old label. After that came (keyboardist) Jan Hammer and (bassist) Rick Laird to do the rehearsal scene with us, as Charlie wasn't doing it. John wanted to form a band with the best musicians he could find and he chose us and we went out on the road. And the rest was history.

GRUBER: There was a perception in the Mahavishnu era that the experience of watching you, the way you played, the way you laid the drums out, the expression on your face, that there was a Billy Cobham look and sound that was uniquely entertaining, even exhilarating. To this day, YouTube video comments talk to that image, "He could power an entire city," "He's a force of nature." What powered those perceptions?

COBHAM: My focusing on not just the sound, but the placement of the instruments, creating a personal sonic community of sound that represented my personality, along with the rudimental patterns I would play. This is where Joni Mitchell and I come together. She would have more than three, maybe up to six guitars on the bandstand, all tuned differently, some with capos, for a specific song. I found it was unique to put the drums in different places and tune them, so when I played a certain piece, I had those pitches close to me. I would be selective, using a multiple tom environment for that purpose. Joe Zawinul asked, why do you play so many drums? I know when I need them. I want them to be available for me when I need them. Not two toms as per a conventional jazz set-up, no, no, no. I'm playing musically, conceptually. Keeping everyone closely knit from not just a rhythmic, but from a melodic and harmonic standpoint, a choice of tones that would draw everyone back into line with what we were doing. It was how we secured, how we approached the development of the rhythmic groove of the band.

GRUBER: Did any of your musical work over the years affect any part of your body? By standing too close to your gongs?

COBHAM: (Indicating hearing aids) That goes there. Those are hearing aids in there. State of the art. For business dealings, I have to wear them.

Otherwise, I go, "'ey? 'ey? 'ey?"

GRUBER: All this time, I never noticed.

COBHAM: Most of the time I forget.

GRUBER: If you're going to be in that business with that amount of sound, especially in the '70's…

COBHAM: Everybody. McLaughlin did play extremely loud.

GRUBER: Why was the volume important? A stereotype would be, if you're studying with Sri Chinmoy, you're meditating, you're into serenity, you wouldn't be the guy pumping up the volume.

COBHAM: Ego. E-G-O. In 1971, we were invited to play at the BBC in Shepherd's Bush in the theater. We were on tour in Europe.

GRUBER: I watched it.

COBHAM: Did you see a guy fall over? These guys came out in white smocks with their clipboards and acoustic checkers to make sure we didn't go over a 90db level. We set up and they were checking levels. The producer instructed John, if you play past 90db, we will stop the show. John looks at him. Behind us, the reason they were concerned, John's amplification alone was 1600 watts, Marshall guitar amps. They were growling like pit bulls. Jerry Goodman had, like, four acoustic, two 360's, two 260's just for violin. We are talking about 1000 watts of power. Jan the same. In the middle of all of that, Rick Laird with 1000 watts of bass amp, with W speakers for sub-wattage. I'm playing what looked like at the time one of the biggest drum sets ever seen. With no muffling. Just drums. The guy had a point. John didn't say anything. And I had the 38-inch gong behind me. At the beginning of the show, John played one chord, from *One Word*, and it was so loud that it threw the cameraman off the dais. *BWAANNGG*!!!! We ended up playing the show, they heavily attenuated us. It had a lot to do with ego.

GRUBER: Chick Corea came to the first shows and said he had never heard anything that loud. It was a common reaction. It was part of the sound and the experience.

COBHAM: We went to Brown University in Providence. They thought they booked an acoustic Indian band for Homecoming. No one paid attention to the Marshall 800 amps.

McLaughlin's guitar rig, Jerry's rig, easily another 500 watts, two stacked amps. Rick Laird had 2,000 watts of bass. Jan had easily two acoustic 360's and one 260 and my drums were behind all that with the gong. And they're thinking they have an Indian band. They were more concerned we started on time. So, we started on time and the first chord was easily between 130 and 140db, you didn't have to turn on the PA. The whole building trembled to its foundations.

GRUBER: That's a great story.

COBHAM: There is a magazine ad of a guy sitting in front of an amp with his hair going back, that was the audience in total. People were talking and John said, now we would like to stop for a moment of prayer, and I am sitting thinking they don't even know what's coming. Next moment, man, he put the guitar up and brought it down and it was like World War III had come to Brown University. They walked out in an absolute daze, and on the floor were so many unconsumed tabs of acid. We were the perfect remedy for anybody's drug problem.

Bill has endless stories about his years touring with the band. Mahavishnu played a Berlin show at Philharmonic Hall in 1973 during a peak period of East-West tensions (Berlin was divided between communist East and capitalist West by its infamous wall). "We were charged by the audience," Bill recalls. One segment of the audience wanted the band to play, the other demanding that they march against the East Germans and the Russians. It was supposed to be a two to three-hour show, on a weekend afternoon. "There were riots in the parking lot." M.O. played only two or three tunes, but were there for hours, trying to find a way out of an increasingly heated political situation. Chants of "Take down the wall" and "Free all political prisoners" interrupted McLaughlin's opening moment of silence as well as the performance itself. Audio techs became the band's bodyguards.

GRUBER: Mahavishnu opened for several progressive rock bands, Yes, Emerson, Lake and Palmer. Keith Emerson took some classical and jazz themes…

COBHAM: No, not a fusion artist, don't know where to place him. What blocked me was that there were so many notes, so much information coming in. Much of it didn't make sense to me. He had a high level of technical proficiency. Didn't get, as in George Benson, the connection, the musical thread, "What are you telling me?" I just left. What I heard was a wall of sound. Amazing, saw all the instruments. This is marketing. Many artists in a position to have this kind of promotion stay in front of the public view not because they have something to say. Their story is not in the music, it's in what people see, the presentation.

GRUBER: ELP with Carl Palmer, Yes with Bill Bruford in big arenas like Madison Square Garden, huge kits, big spectacle.

COBHAM: Right, but see the thing is, in some cases, you luck out and you get a musician, and when you mention Bruford, he is a musician. And has great ideas. He plays with thought, I got it. Anderson singing, the band made sense. Emerson, Lake and Palmer? No, come on, not for me.

There was a small period where interesting quirky acts were being entertained. Zappa was another, for a longer time than us. High-energy stuff. Progressive rock is similar to fusion. The complexity of arrangements, the intensity. Both were powerful, the excitement of something new. There was mutual appreciation. Mixed black and white musicians in the same band. Irish boys got strings, black dudes have West African drum legacy, rhythm section. White man got the schmaltz. There was a release from traditional songs, choruses, a whole departure from what music was. With a fusion band, you get to cut loose, show what you can do. DJs were able to play what they wanted, without record company marketing driving their choices. Then we were gone. We had a shot. I was lucky to be there.

GRUBER: Do you miss Mahavishnu musically?

COBHAM: No, I don't miss it. We did it, it was cool, I enjoyed myself and we moved on. The music that was created by that band, by John McLaughlin was the best I have ever heard him do, except for arrangements of Bill Evans, *Conversations with Myself*. Amazing. In the midst of a major transition, Mahavishnu Orchestra represented the equivalent of 'shock and awe.'

GRUBER: You had all that going on in the culture, Guru Maharaji, Hare Krishna, Sri Chinmoy, Maharishi and here is this marker saying we are different too, and that branding probably helped in the awareness and adoption of Mahavishnu.

COBHAM: We were there for a short period of time, filling a gap. Hendrix is gone, Joplin is gone, the Beatles were disbanding, flower power is turning into something else. Buddhism, new philosophies, people were searching for truth within themselves, their community, they needed something to support them or give them pause to consider on all sides. The sonic side as well.

GRUBER: What was going through your mind when you saw big houses sell out. You were making $500 a week at the time?

COBHAM: When we were working, we got paid for the week. We were working a lot. I don't know what we got for the recording sessions, probably the same 500 bucks. We did that stuff and the money was secondary. When I looked at where we were playing, I understood that somebody was making money. What I had that was special was a steady job. I was comfortable with that. Young? Stupid? Yeah.

In February or March of 1973, John said he would change the band and asked me if I wanted to stay on with him and I said sure. This was a band as I understood from John that was earning $50,000 a night. He was proud of that, rightly so. At least a grand would be cool. But that was a point for me.

I was not a follower of Chinmoy. I got the feeling that either I would have to toe the line or get out. I started to see Narada Michael Walden. I didn't know who he was, but he was in all-white and he would sit behind me, can you imagine, Brian, on stage for concerts. Always smiling. John McLaughlin allowed this.

GRUBER: Why was Narada there?

COBHAM: To. Take. My. Place.

GRUBER: Did you ever consider telling him to get off the stage?

COBHAM: No. I didn't because I understood what was happening. They wanted me to be aggressive because then it was my problem.

GRUBER: Was there a discussion whereby you, Jan Hammer, a couple of the others, could say, 'OK, John, you have harvested a lot of cash in the last year. Critics are claiming that there are five co-equal, masterful musicians, we got something great here and we need to renegotiate this thing.' You were voted the best jazz drummer in the world. Was there discussion that you should give John his due but let's renegotiate billing, ownership, what was paid?

COBHAM: No. Period. That is a very wonderful big fat no to everything you said. Why? Because no one was thinking that way back then. We were young, man. I was speaking for me. (By 1973) I no longer wanted to work for that amount of money. That was when I started to blow my horn about making a record of my own. I am not going to win that war.

No one remembers *Birds of Fire* or anything else compared to *Stratus* or *Red Baron*. And, very few can play that music due to its uniqueness. All I did was give the people what they want. Which is something that John did not like to do. Play something with a groove? No.

I was told everyone in the band received $50,000 as a buyout. I remember very clearly, the last day I spent in Nat Weiss' office, I was given a raise, $1,000 for the week. I had an appointment so I was going to come back to get the check. And then, the next thing I know, when I got there, they said, you're no longer in the band. A piece of paper that said it was over, I was fired. Oh, really?

By then, I had made *Spectrum*. That was starting to ruffle a few feathers.

GRUBER: I would think so. One minute you're his guy, the next you're doing this on your own so you see each other differently.

COBHAM: Yeah, I was more of an adversary then. He let go of Jerry, Rick, and Jan. Jan then got *Miami Vice* through Nat. I did not get any money. It was said I had earned $50,000 over time with my salary so I wasn't supposed to get anything else, this came second-hand. They never talked to me about it.

GRUBER: Why did you do *Spectrum* while still in Mahavishnu? Jan played on the album, so it wasn't a secret to the band. Was McLaughlin concerned as a band leader?

COBHAM: If it did cause friction, I wasn't made aware of it. That band was coming to an end. The reason I was making that record was I had to get out of Dodge with something they couldn't keep away from me. Rick Laird had an opportunity to do what he wanted to do, he had a great eye and chose to become a photographer. He was an untapped source, a great writer and a great orchestrator. Much better than Jan or Jerry. Myself, I came in last because I didn't know anything about it. I struck gold by chance and, I suspect, by being underestimated.

GRUBER: There was controversy around that time (1973, the third and final year of the band), a *Crawdaddy* article that John read on the way to Japan; a couple of the band members, Jan and Jerry were critiquing him for not embracing their compositions as well as the business side. It seems your response was, do your own thing and don't worry about what McLaughlin was allowing you to do.

COBHAM: They had their opportunities. Jan created a perfect avatar in the moog synthesizer that sounded like John. At times, Jan sounded better on the synthesizer than John sounded on the guitar and John took it personally.

Harvey Mason had done it too, choosing his own path. Billy Taylor had his own niche. People who are able to do that are very fortunate.

GRUBER: Did John ever give you feedback on the music in *Spectrum*?

COBHAM: Never ever has he complimented me on the record. The only complimentary thing that John McLaughlin ever gave me was a picture of John Coltrane for Christmas, that I have to this day. What he did in terms of compliments was perform and work with me as a colleague. When we were on stage, we worked together. Clearly the only way the *Mahavishnu Orchestra* would have functioned. In that way, we were a powerful duo, a great collaboration.

GRUBER: Did you ever try to offer any of those original compositions to Mahavishnu?

COBHAM: No, man, I didn't write them at the time. What I did offer was my help in creating new compositions even though I was totally ignorant as to how to write. I would love to collaborate but I didn't have the tools. What I was asking John to do was to teach me how to help create. He wasn't interested.

I didn't start to write music until 1973. With two fingers, like learning how to use a typewriter, like a cub reporter in a newspaper. I didn't really know what to do. I had to make it happen. But out of this negative came a positive. *Heather*, *Spectrum*, *Crosswinds* came from the heart, man, what I was feeling, it was all I could do. I could relate to Ray Charles, "Hit the road, Jack, don't you come back no more." That's reality, that's truth. Music does not lie. Music is the purest form of truth.

"He and My Dad Spent Some Fun Times Together:" The Jan Hammer Interview

Before leaving for London, I stayed in the Carmel, New York home of childhood friend Evan Shatz and wife Joan. Years ago, Evan told me that he had sushi one night with Jan Hammer as their daughters were friends. Evan asked daughter Alissa to write Jan's daughter Jane to set up a possible interview while I was in town. No response.

Then, while in London, Jane writes back. "I don't believe I ever got a chance to meet Bill myself, but the name definitely rings a bell! I know he and my dad spent some fun times together." Yes. Some fun times together. Acknowledging the time zone, I ask Jan for an 8am Eastern Time call, and he jokes he does nothing before 10. On our 10am ET call, Jan's tone throughout was what you might expect, warm, whimsical, modest, enthusiastic, and smart.

GRUBER: Do you remember when you first met Bill?

JAN HAMMER: There was a band called Dreams. I saw them at the Village Gate. The next time, Billy and John came over to jam at our loft on the Lower East Side. There was some talk about making a band out of all this.

GRUBER: Do you recall early intuitions during jamming that something was fresh or unique in some way?

HAMMER: Of course, there was some new angle with the instrumentation, and, for me, the violin; I was so impressed with the combination of sounds. I was used to a trumpet; John's angle into music was so from left field. Over the summer of 1971, when we were rehearsing on Crosby Street, the music started to reach a whole other level by the interplay of all five of us. And there is where I think Bill's sturdy underpinning left me feeling very safe. I knew that he would be there to catch me. Something super special.

GRUBER: What was the crowd reaction for those first shows at the Gaslight (Au Go Go)?

HAMMER: At this point, it's become almost like a legend but I think it's true. I remember we played the first tune at the Au Go Go, and there was total silence for a long time. People were just sitting there with their mouths open. Eventually there was applause, but there was a long delay of complete shock. It was something that I never experienced before.

GRUBER: You contributed to Bill's first album *Spectrum*. I think you'd love to hear the big band horn arrangements on some of those tunes. At the time, you were both still with Mahavishnu, doing a lot of gigs. Why did you choose to do that project with Bill?

HAMMER: He had sketches of his tunes and I was able to help him put a final shape on it. He knew from working together in the band that we could cooperate in that sort of constructive fashion. I knew exactly what he was after. I felt very much part of something really, really interesting. It was a great combination.

GRUBER: Was it well-received by other band members, including John, others branching out and doing something on their own?

HAMMER: I don't remember anything untoward. Billy was the first one. I knew eventually when this thing was over, I was going to go out and do things on my own.

GRUBER: John started the band and played his compositions. Were you and other members of the band interested in playing your own music?

HAMMER: It took a while but eventually we did. I just felt we contributed musically more than we were credited for. It's the hangover from the jazz days, there is a head, and 90 percent of the performance is improvisation and contribution of the players. The music business was not ready to accommodate or acknowledge that. It turned out to be frustrating after a while.

GRUBER: You were playing to large houses at the time.

HAMMER: For the last half year of the band, we were able to participate much more in the success. That's what happens with every band.

GRUBER: Was something of the Mahavishnu style evident in the *Spectrum* recording sessions?

HAMMER: I thought it was quite an interesting and healthy departure into more of a funkier feel instead of the Indian Improvisational Olympics (*laughs*) we were doing on a nightly basis. This was more of a relaxed vision, to have a more groovy mood.

GRUBER: What was Bill's style as a bandleader?

HAMMER: It's funny. I knew it was his record but I didn't see him as a bandleader, I don't recall any kind of a hierarchy at all. There were all kinds of dynamics and cross currents. You could also tell with Jerry, Billy was not able to lock in rhythmically as well as he could with me, not a spoken thing. He wanted me to come in with my skill set to act as an editor, to oversee the form and shape of the tunes.

GRUBER: Do you have a favorite story about Bill, or one that you shouldn't tell?

HAMMER: Billy is a seriously powerful physical specimen of a man. We were in San Francisco at Bill Graham's, I think it was Winterland, and in the dressing room there was a ping-pong table; Bill Graham and everyone played. Jerry and Billy played and Jerry scored one over Billy. So, Billy came and grabbed him and flipped him upside down. It was the funniest thing I have ever seen.

Another time, we were playing in the middle of a super intense tune, Billy shattered a stick and a sharp shard from the stick lodged itself in his forehead. And he kept playing. I remember saying, "Oh my God." That was a legendary Billy Cobham moment.

GRUBER: There is an apocryphal Tommy Bolin story, where he scored a Deep Purple audition because of his solos on *Spectrum*, several of which were yours. Ever heard the story?

HAMMER: That happened with a lot of reviews. It led me to put a disclaimer on my first solo album, 'to those concerned, *there is no guitar on this album*,' in direct response to the Tommy Bolin situation.

Bill told me the story, then Cobham band guitarist Jean-Marie Ecay laughingly insisted it was he who discovered it first, in a magazine interview with Deep Purple's David Coverdale. In the piece, David describes how the band was discussing Jeff Beck and Rory Gallagher as possibilities for a replacement guitarist.

> Then I said Tommy Bolin. They said, "Who?" I said, "I don't know what kind of image this guy has. I've only heard him on Alphonse Mouzon's Mind Transplant album and on Billy Cobham's Spectrum album."
>
> Paicey (drummer Ian Paice) was, of course, a big Billy Cobham fan and he says, "Do you have anything of his?" I went back to my hotel room and came down with a compilation cassette that I'd made and presented this stuff and they said, "Fuck, he's great."
>
> ...I must own up that once I was at a party with Bonzo (Led Zeppelin drummer John Bonham) and Tommy and Spectrum was on the fucking record player. I went, "Oh I love this lick of yours," and Tommy goes, "Oh, that's Jan (Hammer)." I went, "Oh sorry." Then I was going, "Oh, but listen to this one, Tommy. I really love this one." Tommy goes, "That's also Jan, David." I was like, "Oh for fucks sake." [6]

---

[6] Wright, Jeb. "David Coverdale – Returning to the Deep." *Classic Rock Revisited*. http://www.classicrockrevisited.com/show_interview.php?id=1113

GRUBER: When did you first experiment with the moog synthesizer or with the minimoog? Were you influenced by Wendy/ Walter Carlos' work? *A Clockwork Orange* came out the same year Mahavishnu launched.

HAMMER: I was aware of the sound but was not interested so much in the orchestrational quality, the way it was used before. I was more interested in a lead solo instrument. Keith Emerson did a little bit of that but mostly it was used as a sci-fi effect sound. Once I started working with the minimoog, I realized that this could be my voice. And sure enough, that's what happened.

Miami Vice was a smash-hit American TV series produced by film and television director Michael Mann (Manhunter, Heat, Ali, The Insider), featuring Don Johnson and Philip Michael Thomas as detectives working undercover in Miami. It ran from 1984 to 1989 and Hammer's score was considered a key component of its unique aesthetic.

GRUBER: Is it odd for you as a classically trained musician to be known worldwide mostly for a TV theme song?

HAMMER: It's absolutely OK with me. I'm very proud of it. I used all the things I learned in all my disciplines.

GRUBER: Was it unusual at the time for original music to be commissioned for each episode?

HAMMER: I took it very seriously, creating a whole new feel for each episode. People who wrote for dramatic series would basically just do variations on the theme and that would be it every week. It would always sound the same, a certain established tone of the show. I ended up going on all kinds of excursions musically. It was my favorite way of using music. There were these long montages without dialogue and music just takes over and carries the narrative.

GRUBER: Did Michael Mann approach you with a unique vision for the use of soundtracks in the series?

HAMMER: When I met him, the first thing he said to me was he wanted this show to sound unlike anything else on television. So, I figured, that sounds like a job for me (*laughter*).

GRUBER: Tell me about your work with Sarah Vaughan. Why is she so fondly remembered in the jazz world?

HAMMER: She was an unbelievable personality. She was "one of the guys" as they would say. There was no star diva thing happening. You felt totally at home with her. The only time I got spanked was when we did a Johnny Carson *Tonight Show* in New York. I knew I was not going to be on-camera, sitting in the orchestra, so I didn't get dressed, wore a jean jacket, and she gave me a serious dressing-down. From then on, it was tuxedo or nothing.

GRUBER: You did an Amnesty International TV spot that featured Vaclev Havel. Do you think music played an important role in the Czech 'Velvet Revolution?'

HAMMER: It cultivated the soil for it to happen. Things like *Voice of America*, we listened to it every night and taped it, shared tapes and we got to hear all of the beautiful American jazz music. Eventually it was pop music; the Czech people just took to it like fish to water. A lot of talented young musicians came out of that period. Unfortunately, we had to run away in 1968 as things turned out badly. Still, there was definite influence on the culture.

GRUBER: Louis Armstrong and many jazz musicians did U.S.-sponsored tours. Whatever the motivation, altruistic or otherwise, it seems that it did have an impact, particularly in Eastern Europe.

HAMMER: I remember sitting at a Louis Armstrong concert. I was still in high school. Fantastic feeling. There is a definite plus to reaching out and exposing closed societies to something fantastic and world class.

GRUBER: What do you spend most of your time doing these days?

HAMMER: I'm just taking it easy. I live in the country. I am putting together a collection of music for an album with all kinds of beautiful stuff. I did a big anniversary concert with Jeff Beck at the Hollywood Bowl, a highlight of my year. It was great.

Breakups and Reunions

GRUBER: When I talked with Jan this afternoon, he said he was free to experiment because of the foundation you laid down with Mahavishnu.

COBHAM: It wasn't only me, it was me and Rick. You can see it in his face in the videos. Somebody had to do it. Otherwise, it would have been a completely atonal free jazz band. McLaughlin had no sense of time, always getting faster and faster. Reach God as quickly as possible. The problem was the bus only ran so fast so he had to learn how to cope.

He got the best band but intellectuals as well who thought for themselves, who wanted to expand on that concept as a unit. We all wanted to be a part of the project and loved it. And yes, thank you very much, we wanted to be paid for it, not only materially but acknowledged, and that's where there was a problem. To provide acknowledgment meant it was not just John and Sri Chimnoy. Had it been done in that way, the Mahavishnu Orchestra could have lasted 20-30 years, a lot more creative. It would have been a huge library. We would have helped each other.

GRUBER: After the Mahavishnu breakup in 1973, you recorded…

COBHAM: I recorded with John McLaughlin on an album in 1978, one or two tracks. In 1983, 1984, we made a recording called *Mahavishnu*, recorded in France with Bill Evans and others.

GRUBER: After your experience in '73, why do anything with McLaughlin in '78? Didn't it feel a little odd?

COBHAM: Out of respect for the music. That was always the one positive thing that stood out above everything else.

GRUBER: After the 1984 recording session in Paris, you were supposed to go on tour with John as the new Mahavishnu Orchestra, with Bill Evans.

COBHAM: I was trying to find out how I was going to get there, who was going to cover my expenses. Dealt with a guy named Albert Koski, a bunch of gangsters really, in Paris. It was all about who was going to blink first.

Now it's time to prepare to go out on the road. It's approaching the last part of June, 1984, I know that we have concerts that were supposed to be booked. I was so into it, I canceled all my work for the year to put myself in a position to make this happen. I get nothing until a phone call comes from Bobby Liser, who used to be road manager for the Rolling Stones, owned Swiss Cheese and Chocolate Company, supplying many people around Europe with stuff they can't get anywhere else, rare instruments in rock and roll. "Hey Billy, calling to ask, it's the beginning of July, why aren't you here in Montreux? Aren't you playing with the Mahavishnu Orchestra? They are here and Danny Gottlieb is the drummer." McLaughlin was supposed to give me a schedule for rehearsal so we could go on tour. I was bringing my two oldest daughters with me. The shock of my life was, not only was I not there, but that I had been blamed for not being there. That I had backed out.

A few weeks ago, for the first time since then, of all people to come to play in a blues band, opposite the project that I was doing, was Danny Gottlieb. He came and said I always wanted to sit with you and to apologize to you for what happened. They really jerked you around, used you as a scapegoat for the failure of the tour.

GRUBER: What is your interpretation, who thought they could be advantaged by treating you in that way? Was it confusion, lack of organization, incompetence, was it malicious?

COBHAM: I believe it was malicious, I believe he has an ego problem. I believe he wanted to try to make me look bad. The reason, I was the guy in the band that no one expected anything from. I was just a drummer in the band. I wanted to contribute and do my part. I didn't argue, Jerry Goodman, Jan Hammer, they were the chief talkers to John. The body language was confrontation almost all the time. This was about who was the alpha. It's something I don't have to prove. I'm looking to play the best I can on my instrument. He chose to use me as a scapegoat based on the fact that he could not make me subservient. I was not beholden to him for anything. He could not argue with me about funds.

When Gottlieb told me the story, it corroborated everything I had thought had happened. To the point that we were laughing about the fact that we were both given a bad review by a highly respected *New York Times* music critic – he sent somebody else and he didn't get the names right. I was told a reason why the tour didn't go down so well was that people kept screaming for "Billy! Billy! Billy!"

GRUBER: The *New York Times* reviewer criticized your drumming and you weren't even there.

COBHAM: And playing percussion with Danny Gottlieb when Danny was actually the drummer.

"I Know Some Tunes:" Cobham and McLaughlin at Montreux

GRUBER: Why did you agree to do the 2010 duet with John at Montreux?

COBHAM: Because (Montreux co-founder and impresario) Claude Nobs asked me to.

GRUBER: In the sessions with you and John for the two weeks before Mahavishnu formed, plus perhaps the session in Montreux, was there was a certain energy that was unique or memorable for you?

COBHAM: We didn't talk much. We just played. That's why in Montreux the duet worked so easily. We just fell back into what we did when we started. He played, I listened. I played with him and supported him. He had a strong overall rhythmic value sense of how he wanted to present his ideas. This was not about playing fast or slow. Yeah, as far as I was concerned, his control of tempo was not very good but I could work with him. If he got faster, we got faster together. That's it. And he never got slower. So, wherever we went, we went together, because I knew how to control and treat that aspect of the music that we created as a duet. That's something that we developed before there was a Jan Hammer, Jerry Goodman, or Rick Laird, so that when they came in, that foundation was already set.

GRUBER: People raved about it musically. What was that experience for you emotionally?

COBHAM: The one thing that got me a little bit upset for a split second was a claim he made that my ability to hold time was bad. And I just went, really? After all these years? I knew where the problem always sat was completely opposite. I realized this guy is still very much insecure about a lot of things. I rarely complemented John on anything he did. I didn't think I had to. He played his ass off. Some situations would happen where he did something really special. Those situations reflected feeling. Not speed, a million notes a bar. The right notes within the bar that were necessary. I loved the ballads. I loved all the material but, *A Lotus on Irish Streams*, when he played what he was feeling, I would have to come to him and say, that's beautiful.

GRUBER: Montreux is only 100 kilometers from your home in Schupfen, Switzerland. How was it that Claude reached out to you to come to Montreux at the last minute for the encounter with John?

COBHAM: Montreux is jazz only in name. Jazz is important because it is an art form that is supported by Swiss law, folkloric. If you put jazz in, they will put in quite a few hundred thousand bucks to support the festival. It's jazz but nobody is playing jazz. Herbie is doing *Rock It*. Nobs said we need you to come and play. "There is an act in Canada, Toronto with a hit record, we asked them to come and perform at Montreux. They agreed but their office thought that the spelling of the venue city was a mistake for the spelling of Montreal." (*Laughter*) Right, uh huh. This was a project that was supposed to happen on a Saturday. That meant that they had to take the flight from Toronto to get to Geneva the night before, then drive to Montreux the following day. Needless to say, they went to take a flight to Montreal on the same day the gig was supposed to happen.

I asked Claude, "What do you want to do?" He said, I want you to play with John. I said, no. He said I have got an open check, you put the number in yourself. He said it's Stravinsky Hall and Bryan Ferry (Roxy Music) is not going to sell out that hall alone. Well, me and John McLaughlin got on the bandstand, we were supposed to play for 25 minutes, we ended up playing for 45 minutes, because they would not let us off the stage as a duet. I played on whatever they had. I had to pick and choose and put something together. John had no guitars, no picks, he came on vacation with his son and wife. I said to McLaughlin, hey, what do you want to play. He said, "I know some tunes." That was his response. (*Laughter*) Really. "You know some tunes that I know from Mahavishnu Orchestra." He said I know the beginning and I know the end but I don't know anything in the middle.

(*Laughter*) It's true, Brian. I said, "Let's see how far we get."

GRUBER: Were there conversations in recent years with John about reassembling some version of Mahavishnu?

COBHAM: There were all kinds of rumors. Nothing ever came to be. What I believe happened had more to do with the relationship with Jan Hammer. The only way that the band could happen is if all of the original members were there. We could not get away with not having Rick. At one point, Rick had not played a bass on the road for almost 20 years. John had a problem with Jan as his synthesizer sounded so much like John's guitar. That was one musical problem. Jan had built that sound because that is what he wanted to do. Tommy Bolin, when he got the gig with Deep Purple, what they thought they heard as guitar solos, that was Jan Hammer. Jan was the spitting musical image of John. Except for one thing. Jan had a great sense of timing, in terms of how he played certain figures. But then, to me, Jan was the best all-around musician in the band. Played great drums, was influenced by Elvin Jones, great piano player and keyboardist, wonderful knowledge of violin and string instruments. What more could you want? He was the perfect guy to put everything together. He was the glue. John had the image and of course his musical prowess was unquestioned. The material and the ideas, no problem.

Rick was very unique in that someone had to play simple. Someone had to just lay it down, some cornerstone. He was it. Jerry Goodman was the last person I garnered respect for, it took me years to figure out how he fit in musically. God willing, I am 73 and just got my head wrapped around it in the last few years. There were a lot of notes that didn't seem to make sense until recently, man, sounds wonderful. Why I neglected to focus on Jerry was my being immature, not really being able to put things in place with that band, who did what and how it clicked. I have a better understanding of that now. It took me years to understand what John Coltrane did on records. An unbelievable amount of information coming from him. Layers of it, same thing for M.O., same thing for Jimi Hendrix. Maybe if I am around another 10 or 20 years, I'll become a Zappa fan.

The Rock and Roll Collaborations

GRUBER: Tell me how you met (*Spectrum* guitarist) Tommy Bolin.

COBHAM: Smiled all the time. Music was his playground. When he expressed himself, it was from the heart, from beyond, like some older beings took his place. He died at 27. Met him when he was 19. Played guitar at a NASCAR racetrack in the Carolinas. Dreams, 1969-70, saw him play. Big festival. Me and Michael and Randy Brecker, (guitarist John) Abercrombie. (Tommy's band) Zephyr was the opening act. We were probably second, followed by, I believe, Fleetwood Mac or Grand Funk Railroad. He did something with the Echoplex no one had heard before. He uses it before my drum solo into *Red Baron*. I realized that this was the beginning of an era. Played guitar with one hand, playing tap guitar. Guy in Italy in 1965 did it first.

GRUBER: How did the (1973) *Love Devotion Surrender* project with Carlos Santana come together? Jan Hammer was involved as well as John (McLaughlin).

COBHAM: Carlos had this incredible guitar sound and still does. For rock and roll, for a lead guitar player, *wooooo*, off the hook. He played what he felt. It tells the story of what is popular, what people want to hear and feel. He found his niche. Carlos loved what John was doing. What John did was the result of a lot of years of creativity. What Carlos did have was a huge audience. John wanted that and rightly so, it's a business. They needed a rhythm section with consistency to give them some foundation. They never did get that together. They were not willing to share more than what they offer to make the music really stick. A lot of marketing and it got them over.

GRUBER: You assembled something of a rock fusion all-star group *Alivemutherforya* in the late seventies, with Tom Scott on sax, Mark Soskin, keyboards, Alphonso Johnson on bass, and Steve Khan, son of the great lyricist Sammy Cahn, on guitar. You later joined Jack Bruce and Friends for a year. Jack was most famous as part of the seminal rock trio Cream. Was it a rock and roll band? And, why do it?

COBHAM: Rock, but also rock fusion. Jack called me up and said I'd like you to join me. I was always a big fan of Jack's voice. He just sang with reckless abandon, had this wonderful pure sound. Wasn't a baritone, wasn't a tenor. He always represented to me this truth, like he was yelling the truth through every word.

GRUBER: Were you a fan of Cream?

COBHAM: No, not at all. I wasn't interested. It all sounded produced, created by someone behind the scenes, a marketing vehicle. They looked like they sounded good. One of the things I got about The Beatles was that they had imagination. They had a story, it came in the lyrics, they spoke and dressed a certain way. A message with a lineage. If you put them up to American players, they couldn't hold a candle. They had to come over to the States to learn how to play the blues. Clapton (Bill mentions later that he was a fan of Derek and the Dominos) came over and his influence was B.B. King and it gave him a certain personality. With Cream, if it wasn't for Jack Bruce and the way he presented his ideas, I don't think they would ever be acclaimed. Drummer (Ginger Baker) was about how he looked, banging and keeping time, but then where is the music really coming from. (Jack was) beyond any male voice at the time.

GRUBER: Jack came from a jazz background.

COBHAM: The Scottish jazz scene. He just presented me with this very clear *'in your face, this is who I am and this is how I feel'* presentation. I wanted to be involved with him. I wanted to play some rock to play with people I could support and also learn from. In rock and roll when you play with people like that and you come from a different background, you tend to try to fit in. It was pretty easy with Jack.

GRUBER: How much of an adjustment was it to play with Jack?

COBHAM: Very much of an adjustment because I had to play only what was necessary. Power down, if you will. Not fill in gaps unless it was required or asked of me. What I needed to play, in as musical a way as possible, was a groove. Rock and roll is coming from a perspective of, just what people needed, how they felt, how they moved, just as if it were in the blues, or in gospel, dance. They wanted something they could connect their bodies with. So that every beat was like how they moved. That meant it had to be simple and direct and to the point. So, if it was a very slow ballad and it was in three, it was like one, two, three, *boom*, every time, but it had to feel as if something human, not mechanical. People like Chuck Berry, B.B., James Cotton, they had that because that's all they knew. That's what music was to them. Someone gave it a title, and that title gave it certain marketing parameters.

GRUBER: What did Jack ask of you?

COBHAM: Play on a record and tour, sometime around 1980/81. Jack Bruce and Friends. One record, called *I've Always Wanted to Do This*. We toured Europe, were on a bill with Sting and The Police in Essen, Germany at the Rockpalast. Jack was a big Charlie Parker fan and wrote this thing called *Bird Alone* and it's one of the most intense rock and roll, fusion - whatever you want to call it - tunes I have ever played. He was playing piano, then he picked up his bass and he was like a bull in a china shop. And singing. Wow, man, it was one of the great moments for me with Jack Bruce. David Sancious, original E Street Band, plays keyboards and double-necked blues guitar, and Clem Clempson from Colosseum and Humble Pie was the regular guitarist, four of us. I had a ball. It was a great time to learn to respect the rock scene. To work with Jack, then turn around and work with Bob Weir, Bobby and the Midnites. It was time to suck it up and learn. Played with Bobby Cochran, Alphonso Johnson was in the band at the time, Brent Mydland was there for a split second, organist and keyboardist for the Grateful Dead. We went to Jamaica as opening act for the Dead. That was off the hook crazy. That's when I learned that you just don't drink the punch.

GRUBER: How did Jazz Is Dead come about?

COBHAM: That was in the '90s. Amazing band. The term 'Jazz is Dead' gained the ire of the jazz community. You can understand it. Started with the late T. Lavitz who was in a band called Mother's Finest, keyboard player. Alphonso Johnson, Jimmy Herring, guitar. Bob Weir wrote some really hip things for The Dead but they weren't playing them live because it wasn't in their wheelhouse; complicated pieces like *Franklin's Tower* that they created and put on their records but, I was told, took months to put together. An ingenious, great idea. Took some organizing, took us a couple of days to rehearse, then we went out and played it. The Grateful Dead had

50,000-70,000 people who followed them to the ends of the earth. No big deal to attract 5,000-10,000 just to hear those tunes that the Dead didn't play. It was a very unique thing that we did. I loved it.

GRUBER: Play any of your music?

COBHAM: At some point, they did *Stratus* and *Red Baron*.

GRUBER: Was it jazz?

COBHAM: The Dead wrote it as their spin on jazz but it had a backbeat.

GRUBER: I can see where people thought you were a heretic. Was that part of your identity, part of your experience back then, or an outcome of the experimentation you did, perhaps not appreciated by some people in the jazz community?

COBHAM: Gee, I don't know. You know why? Hey, I'll tell you. Maybe there was a callousness about me, I really didn't give a shit about what other people thought. Because I never thought they thought anything about me. They did not include me in their community and I guess I turned off to that because I didn't fit the resume. I don't do drugs. So, therefore, I didn't hang out with them because I knew it was a closed community. Either you were part of it or you were outside of it. I never gave it a second thought. What was important to me was the end product. How did we play together? Did I enjoy the experience of working with other musicians, no matter what they did? Because once I played on the bandstand with them and we gained acknowledgement for what we did as a unit, I walked off the bandstand, I walked to my room, I closed the door and I was in my own personal cocoon. I didn't bother anybody. I'd get something to eat alone. I'm here to play. The main objective to me, Brian, is to make good music with people I am working with. If it doesn't work, I'm gone.

GRUBER: Is one dimension of that issue that you have all these white artists ripping off the likes of Chuck Berry, maybe getting more notoriety, making more sales; is there built-in resentment, you are playing with people they consider inferior?

COBHAM: No. I played with people I felt comfortable with. Jack played with Tony Williams Lifetime. Jack was the voice of rock-and-roll for me.

Working with Weir, I loved his arrangements. A great salute to work on material for him. That whole bit with Zappa to me was not Zappa. It was about the marketing apparatus behind him. All part of the divide and conquer scene. Looks as if it is a racial question but it is coming from the 1.6 percent of the world that has control over everything material. Then they have to find a way to transfer that concept to artists.

What I realized is it's not about how much money you have in the bank. You are rich because you have access to getting the things you need to survive, something to eat, roof over your head, and a low-stress-level way to live so you can be creative. If you can do that…

GRUBER: Was there a time working with Bruce, Weir, Mahavishnu, where you were thinking, this rock-and-roll world is where I want to play out my career?

COBHAM: No. For me, it was great to watch and I wish I could have done it with one or two more individuals. Male, would have been Peter Gabriel. Female? I would have loved to work with Joni Mitchell. I love what she did. I love those two musical approaches in rock. They felt home to me, a lot of imagination put into why things were happening the way they were.

I was on a (Gabriel) record called *Passion*, (soundtrack for) *The Last Temptation of Christ*, the Scorcese movie. Then I toured with him in 1994, we toured Israel, all kinds of stuff. I loved working with him. We did make another record, the *Big Blue Ball*.

GRUBER: In that era, there was something that attracted you to these rock and roll guys and that world. The financial opportunity, the people, the audiences, the shows, the music, the venues?

COBHAM: It was the music. And I have to go back to one thing you said about the money. There was no money in it for me. The manipulation of the artists by those in management was tremendous, man, in terms of what was promised to musicians. One of the reasons I didn't work with Weir past a specific point was I could not profit on a business level. There was always a loophole. You could get this amount of money but 'maybe we'll make more money so you might get more… or… maybe less.' Someone would sell you on something that had more holes than Swiss cheese. You realize, this guy thinks that I'm really stupid. The road manager is focusing on the main guy in the band. It's not the musician with the name on the marquee but the people who control the artist. They are seeking to keep as much as possible for themselves *and then* for the artist they represent. It's like pulling teeth; you have to wait to be paid for services rendered based on a verbal agreement. They keep all of the money as long as possible and pay as little as possible to the supporting artists, if they can't make them understand that they should be honored working with the star. The artist with the name on the marquee gets blamed for it.

What I got out of playing with these guys was to do my part the best way I could; because my one weapon was my ability to play and to be committed fully musically to the scene at that time. And if I played well, more than likely what was coming to me was not money per se but people remembering that I played my ass off. And the band sounded good because of what I did.

GRUBER: Also, an opportunity to expand your potential market and introduce your music to new fans?

COBHAM: Yes. Absolutely. Unequivocally.

GRUBER: You jammed with the Grateful Dead and with members of the band in several projects.

COBHAM: There was a group of percussionists, Mickey Hart and Bill Kreutzmann, and they would invite Zakir Hussain, Flora Purim, Airto Moreira, myself, others and they called it the Diga Rhythm Band. A lot of drummers, singers. Sometimes we would do things on the road. I did it at Radio City and also *Saturday Night Live* upstairs in the same building.

In that building is a television recording studio, we were in Studio G or H, we were documenting *Saturday Night Live*. In the middle of all that, I had to go downstairs and play on this one tune with the Dead. It was off-the-hook crazy. It was the one time in a 10-block radius that the New York City Police Department employed only policemen who were Deadheads.

The audience? What can you say? People jumping up and down. One of the things that always fascinated me about that band, they are just shuffling down the road and its grooving but no one is dancing in time, they are all in their own zone. When you watch, you think this is wrong, anything that *should* be in synch is completely *out* of synch, it's chaotic movement. They are all having a ball, but I just don't get it. I am going up and down with the band and no one else is doing that.

GRUBER: I saw a hilarious Bobby & The Midnites music video.

COBHAM: I did that out of love for that band. The band for me was rocking. The closest I ever came to country music. It was not in my wheelhouse. The singers in country have their own blues to talk about. As a Latino, I am not familiar with that, I am out of my element. (We find the YouTube video and watch the open together).

It's on a... wow... on the roof of a house, in Brooklyn. Guess what? That record sold over 250,000 units. That's the singer. Bobby Cochran, from Steppenwolf, Eddie Cochran was his uncle, famous musician. That whole scene is pure southern country rock. The bass player Ken Gradney played with Little Feat, been there for 20, 30, 40 years, from New Orleans. That Grateful Dead spin-off band, in essence, that band could easily play a 30-40 city tour because it had Bob Weir's face on it. I don't have that kind of support, so it's on me.

GRUBER: I saw the video of you jamming with the Dead. Miles performed with the Dead at the Fillmore West (after) *Bitches Brew*. Was there something in the ether back then where jazz and rock artists...

COBHAM: Miles was only the opening act, he had nothing to do with them. Don't even go there. The Grateful Dead had a high regard for all music, what they were doing was a small micro-bit of jazz. They had the looks, the right marketing appeal. Someone handling that. Looking like the bad boys. They maintained themselves and were very clever people.

GRUBER: Were you impressed with their music?

COBHAM: I was impressed with their management and the way that they organized things. Ten years before Napster, they were selling product away from the record business. Dick's Picks. Every Dead concert, they had 70,000 people. They had a system where someone could plug into the board. Cassette. They would send in to Dick and he listened and they put it out and these guys would get five dollars a pop.

GRUBER: I was watching videos of your former partner George Duke. And was listening to his sometime bandleader and collaborator Frank Zappa. Did you respect Zappa as a jazz artist or a guitar player?

COBHAM: I didn't hear enough to draw a conclusion except that he looked like a marketing scheme to me. Knowing the people behind him, they saw a bull to take to market and exploit. When you heard him speak, he was eloquent, had interesting ideas. The music to me was not my cup of tea just because it didn't groove, give me a chance to move and feel good. It came at a very good time. Mahavishnu was around but Zappa was there first. He came in the wake of Jimi Hendrix. Hendrix played from the heart, *"This is what I have."* Zappa came with an academic approach to music, everything in its place, vis-a-vis 'the black page,' covered with notes, "Wow, how do you play that??" Everyone forgot to ask what do those notes represent. This guy with the goatee and long hair had a wonderful and effective image, the mad scientist. Someone has to do it. Does it all make sense? No, not to me but maybe to somebody else. So, you listen and think, maybe I'll take a tab of acid and it'll make sense.

GRUBER: There were the earlier Mothers of Invention years with George Duke and then there was the *Hot Rats*, *Peaches en Regalia* jazz-oriented stuff.

COBHAM: I can't refer to anything that he did because the door never opened for me there. Like (Zappa drummer), Terry Bozzio, 64 drums, 16 bass drums, 100 and something cymbals, and you see this amazing monument to God knows what and he is actually playing them. It's not like this is a joke. What is lost on people is the music he is playing on those drums alone. What stays with people is how many drums and cymbals are there. You have this image of complexity. He played some pretty hip stuff on those drums melodically. The little I saw of Zappa, he had (electric violinist Jean-Luc) Ponty in the band, great musician. He conducted the band and took rehearsals to another level. It is music that is not long-lasting. You will not sing too many of Zappa's tunes walking down the street. All due respect, amazing stuff, very complicated.

GRUBER: Last year, you mentioned someone was trying to organize a tour with you and (Yes frontman) Jon Anderson.

COBHAM: I made a recording on a series of compositions that Jon had recorded in Florida a year ago, around spring 2016. We were supposed to do stuff together again. It's not happening. I got paid, I'm gone. Other person might have been Rick Wakeman.

GRUBER: What kind of music?

COBHAM: His music. Jon is a great lyricist; he is a good poet. The thread of music, it's got body to it. It's got something you can grasp. It's a story. It was very easy to support it. The lines were very clear. So, the groove is very easy to access and play along with. What Jon wants you to do is to move and feel good. To dance, even if it's a ballad. To show that it is an infectious theme. That's what to me music should always be about. It's not easy, especially when you come up with geniuses like Keith Emerson who clearly is an amazing musician. It's just channeling all of that information so that I can understand it, for me. I'm simple, man, give me a theme and elaborate on it.

Backstage Wednesday Night

GRUBER: How did you feel about last night's show?

COBHAM: We're getting there.

GRUBER: Standing ovation at the end and the band seemed more relaxed, like they were having fun.

COBHAM: I'm becoming more comfortable in setting things up for them, and they are becoming more comfortable in the way I set things up for them. (Guy enters the room). *You're here!*

BARKER: I have been here for a while.

COBHAM: I want to record the band. (*Describes his equipment to Guy.*)

Guy tells a joke. "A guy goes into a library, 'I'd like a hamburger and fries, two lots…'"

I'm not sure why but I am spellbound by Guy's standup comedy style. Every backstage joke slays me. Is it his delivery? Confidence? Does the star power he exudes onstage carry to his storytelling pre- and post-show?

BARKER: We will do the first thing first set, and then the second set we will do like we did last night but we will substitute *Cap Breton* for *Sal Si Puedes*.

COBHAM: We should work out what we are going to do when we have two 75-minute sets.

GRUBER: You can write something new.

COBHAM: NO!

BARKER: *(Phone rings)*. Hello Mum. Yeah, hang on. I'll call you back, Mum.

GRUBER: Do you communicate anything to the members of the rhythm section or the band after the first two shows?

COBHAM: No. It's direction by way of the music not by way of speaking anymore. It's about phrasing. I played some shit yesterday, just wanted to check it out and see what would happen. And the reason why it works is because I can hear them, and I can play it synchronously inside what was happening already, so everybody is still doing their stuff and I am playing on top of it. In essence, what is happening more and more for me is, I am able to play the drums, and not keep time for them.

GRUBER: Do you have any plan tonight as to what you will try?

COBHAM: Not a clue. Walked on the bandstand yesterday, man, and couldn't hear the drums at all for the first two tunes. I had no body, no security. I told Santiago to tell them. The drums came up, I felt much more comfortable. The tenor saxophone closest to me was blowing my head off because he put the microphone in his saxophone bell, now it's isolated so all you are getting is his saxophone more than anyone in his section. When you hear things out of perspective, you play that way.

GRUBER: Do you have a different plan for Friday and Saturday because you are doing two sets? Different physical preparation?

COBHAM: That's what we were just talking about. Tomorrow is the last day to test all the shit. Now we have to figure out what to do for 75 minutes, probably an extra-long drum solo somewhere in the middle, I don't know, we've got more than enough, 110 minutes' worth of material. So, some things may get repeated. Which is OK too because every time we play it gets better. It should not be difficult in terms of the notes; it should be in terms of the physical stamina sustained.

With the *M.O.* for a while it was very difficult to play long shows. When we got used to it, it felt strange to play shows that were only 45 or 50 minutes long. People used to get very upset with McLaughlin because he didn't give a shit, he played longer. I was so tired sometimes, I would sleep on a ballad and no one would even miss me *(laughter)*. He is playing banjo on *Lotus on an Irish Stream* or something *(snoring sound)* and he would turn around and go "Billy!" and I would go "*What?*"

GRUBER: I was reading Herbie Hancock's autobiography at the train station last night and he said Miles would go out for a cigarette during a jam and one time he came back and asked Herbie's brother, "By the way, what song were we playing?"

COBHAM: Yes. Yes. The solos were so long. God bless Ron Carter, he played a million choruses supporting people. That's why he hated to do uptempo tunes. Same format all the time and nobody could hear him. He was playing acoustic bass, and Tony is just *LAMBASTING* the drums right next to him. Ron could only hear his bass by putting his ear to the fingerboard because no microphone is picking that shit up. His bass mic is picking up the drum set next to him.

Ronnie Scott's Bar Encounter: Mark Mondesir

At the bar Wednesday night, I am introduced to the fellow sitting next to me, who happens to be bassist Michael Mondesir's brother Mark, an accomplished drummer. I thought it would be impressive bar chatter to mention in passing that I spoke to Jan Hammer earlier in the day. Mark responds that he performed with Jan and Jeff Beck at Royal Albert Hall.

MARK MONDESIR: For Jeff's 60th birthday (2004), we played on the 23rd and 24th of June. It was our mother's birthday on the 23rd, so we brought her down, and Jeff's birthday was on the 24th. It was part of an eight-date tour, so we went to Manchester, Bristol, *dadadadada*. It wasn't intended to be a tour. Jeff was doing a project with a string quintet and he invited me on board. Then he said he was missing bass so I got Michael on board. We did not so much rehearse but we had a bit of a jam at Jeff's house for a couple of days.

GRUBER: As one would do. *Why not?*

MONDESIR: We stopped (at Jeff's house) overnight, because we played on the Tuesday and the Wednesday. After the rehearsal, later that evening, we got into a music listening fest. Jeff was playing all kinds of vinyls and we got into what we called a "Jan Hammer Fest." We were playing all these albums, some of which featured Jeff, but Mahavishnu and aspects of Jan's solo work as well. We sat there going mad over his playing and miming every note. Then a week or so later my phone rings and it's Jeff. He says, I hope you're sat down, I just got off the phone to Jan and I told him about you and Mike and he is going to be on a plane. This is, bearing in mind, Jeff and Jan had not played together in 20 years and Jan hardly goes out anyway. It was something of a surreal honor.

GRUBER: No kidding. Great story.

MONDESIR: We started rehearsing at Music Bank studios in south London. Mike and I walk in and already Jeff is there and Jan is there with his keyboard. He already was working on his sound, we rehearsed more and more, Jan would tweak his sound after each concert. It would be just like playing on *Wired* and *There and Back*.

GRUBER: I must ask you. You had the 'Jan Hammer Fest' and played with Jan, presumably including *Spectrum*. Tonight, you see Jan's improvisations from his work with Bill arranged for a big band. How did that impress you?

MONDESIR: Well, I'm always impressed with Guy Barker so it was a lovely surprise but not surprising to know that he took that tack, taking a section of Jan's solo and making it part of the arrangement.

GRUBER: What impact has Bill had on your career or concept as a percussionist?

MONDESIR: Man, well, I always tell people, and I remind Bill whenever I can, quite truthfully, that it is because of him and because I discovered who Billy Cobham was when I was in my mid-teens. It started with a friend of a neighbor who was a rock guitarist. He was the one to tell me and Michael this legend about this guy called Billy Cobham from the United States with '*arms like tree trunks.*' That is exactly what he said. It was almost as if it was some kind of folklore legend. We were like *ooooooh*! In the days of vinyl, we would go to Tower Records and Virgin and HMV, and three local record libraries. Then I see a live album called *Shabazz* from 1974, made up of two concerts, one from the Montreax Jazz Festival and the other from the Rainbow Theatre in London. I took it home and put it on the turntable and the first few bars, Michael was downstairs in the kitchen, and I shout out from the top of the stairs, "*MICHAEL, COME UP HERE,*" because neither of us had heard anything like it. I was into playing drums sort of as a hobby. Both me and Michael were into visual arts. I decided from that moment on I was going to devote my time to learning the drum set as an art form in a complete sense rather than only to play the drums keeping time in a groove-orientated song or concept. Billy was the first person I heard that had used dynamics in terms of volume range, his phrasing was amazing, his ideas, his sense of melody.

After the show, Mark follows up with a coda to our conversation via Facebook.

MONDESIR: Something else I neglected to say, in addition to how Billy's playing inspired me, is how his phrasing is Caribbean and is similar in vibe to the calypso music Mike and I grew up with. The earlier music of The Mighty Sparrow being a classic example. So even within Mahavishnu, his flavour is very Caribbean.

My family are from St. Lucia. Mike told me years ago that Billy has St. Lucian history in his roots. Born in the UK in the mid-60s, I was weaned on incredible music, from everything in the charts at the time, to the Caribbean music my parents brought back and played at home. Calypso rhythmic phrasing is so much more magical and looser than what's found in much 'western' music. Much of it can't be transcribed so it's down to interpretation.

4 RONNIE SCOTT, 52ND STREET AND THE LEFT BEHIND SNARE DRUM

You can get to Ronnie Scott's from several London Underground stops.

Coming from suburban Beaconsfield, a guest of long-time friend and colleague Richard Carter, I transfer each day from Chiltern Railways at Marylebone, then shuttle through one or two Tube lines to Piccadilly Circus. If you stop for a rest in the charming Soho Square Gardens, you're just one and a half blocks away, right down Frith Street. Approaching a club like Ronnie's or New York's iconic Village Vanguard is akin to approaching a favorite cathedral or grand library. Thousands of transcendent moments already in the bank, more served up daily.

Ronnie Scott's sports a red neon sign, *'open nightly'* in green with its iconic blue neon saxophone noting *'hours 6pm to 3am.'* The club has a superb menu though there are plenty of quality watering holes and eateries to sample before or after the show. Just next door is Ceviche Soho, a Peruvian kitchen with a Pisco bar, or wander into Lobo's for tapas. On the club's left is Zima, 'Russian Street Food and Bar', and the Delhi Brasserie flogs superior tandoori. Next to a stage door directly across from the street is Little Italy, fronting four streetside two-tops with white tablecloths. Bar Italia, a popular band hangout, promises caffe espresso, also presenting several tables in front, British football on the telly inside near a display of pastries and sandwiches. Might not be very stylish for you to hang out at a chain restaurant, but Caffé Nero, the Italian coffee company, is right on the corner, with plenty of tables, working wifi and a serviceable bathroom in a pinch. On the other corner is Balans Soho Society Café for fish and chips, Cornish crab linguine, and buttermilk fried chicken. You can experience transcendent music and pull in 4,000 surplus calories, all in one night.

Ronnie Scott on 52nd Street

Ronnie Scott's story doesn't start in 1965 at 47 Frith Street, nor in 1959 at the club's original 39 Gerrard Street location. It starts shortly after World War II, with Scott, an up-and-coming 20-year-old tenor saxophonist walking 52nd Street, known to jazz fans worldwide simply as 'The Street.'

Scott, who passed away in 1996 at the age of 69, is revered as one of Britain's all-time great horn players. As a young man, he couldn't see American bands due to protective restrictions set by the Musicians' Union. Even recordings were difficult to come by due to the high cost of vinyl 'imports.'

Scott took gigs on transatlantic cruises to get to New York and was transfixed by what he saw. 52nd Street had supplanted Harlem's 133rd Street as 'Swing Street' by the mid-30s, and was the premiere spawning ground of new jazz forms and late-night jams until its gradual decline in the '50s and '60s. The last club to close was the Hickory House, featuring Dr. Billy Taylor on piano and a young army drummer named Billy Cobham.

I visited 52nd Street on my way to London, walking the blocks that once teemed with raucous crowds bar-hopping the basement clubs. New York hospitality workers are notorious for knowing city history but the security guards, bartenders and restauranteurs on 52nd knew nothing of the street's pedigree. To while away the late-night hours before my flight, my pal Erik Herz and I hopped a subway to Small's in the West Village, the best place to see the city's elite players jam nightly till the wee hours. After greeting club owner Spike Wilner at the far end of the bar, we settled in for hours of New York's finest after-hours jazz. Intimacy is understating the experience in the 60-seat capacity basement room; I worried about getting my teeth knocked out by a trombone while sitting in the front row.

The two-block stretch of 52nd Street between Fifth and Seventh avenues that mesmerized Scott boasted dozens of packed clubs. You could sample popular, familiar bands or push the envelope for something a little different. Distinctions between styles such as Dixieland, swing, and bebop, often defined along racial lines, were dissolving.

'The Street' was convenient to musicians backing Broadway plays; it was even home to a CBS recording studio. Early evening, you played for others. Round midnight, you came here to play for yourself.

Scott stayed for two weeks during his first-time pilgrimage to New York's jazz scene.

> *There was one especially memorable night when Ronnie Scott heard the great Charlie Parker Quintet with Miles Davis at the Three Deuces. Playing next door was the Dizzy Gillespie Big Band and, late into the night, Davis sat in and blew with Gillespie. The atmosphere was electric and Ronnie Scott carried on dreaming his dreams of setting up a similar kind of club in London.* [7]

You could go see Billie Holiday, Marian McPartland, Louis Prima, Art Tatum or Fats Waller. Erroll Garner and Coleman Hawkins got their start on those sidewalks. Bessie Smith performed on 'The Street,' as did Count Basie, Sarah Vaughan, the Dorsey Brothers, Artie Shaw, even Thelonious Monk who wrote the *52nd Street Theme*, later recorded and performed by Ronnie back home. Live broadcasts from the street enhanced its legendary status throughout the States.

Variety editor Abel Green called it "America's Montmartre." One other thing Ronnie noticed. Comedy till then was largely a jokey, predictable collection of slapstick gags. But New York comedy, from The Street to The Village to the Catskills, offered a new stand-up style that was spontaneous, edgy, sometimes subversive. Alan King and Joey Adams started their careers on The Street, and the tradition of comedy as jazz warmup permeated the metro area. Mort Saul, Woody Allen, Dick Gregory, Lenny Bruce, there was an attitude crossing over the two entertainment genres: inventive, defiant of conventions, daring. Scott, born into an East London

---

[7] www.ronniescotts.co.uk/static/assets/ronnie_scotts_history.pdf

Jewish family, picked up inspiration for his comedy shtick along with his tenor chops and proprietor concepts.

Previously a hang-out for taxi drivers and gamblers, the plan was to convert the Gerrard Street basement into a place where British jazz musicians could jam. In a 1959 feature story on the club's opening, Scott declares to British music weekly *Melody Maker* that he intends to make his club a destination for serious jazz performing and consuming as, "too many clubs degenerate into 'jiving palaces' where it is difficult to appreciate what is happening on the stage. Here there will be plenty of room to dance, but also plenty of room to sit and listen - and see the musicians." [8]

A small ad in *Melody Maker* announces the grand opening performance:

> *Tubby Hayes Quartet; the trio with Eddie Thompson, Stan Roberts, Spike Heatley. A young alto saxophonist, (club co-founder) Peter King, and an old tenor saxophonist, Ronnie Scott. The first appearance in a jazz club since the relief of Mafeking by Jack Parnell.* [9]

For the uninitiated, Parnell was a British jazz drummer and bandleader, with Mafeking an offbeat reference to the seven-month siege of a British-held town during South Africa's Second Boer War. Also for the uninitiated, Eddie Thompson played with Billy at the Hickory House when he subbed for Billy Taylor.

"I love this place, it's just like home, filthy and full of strangers." – Ronnie Scott

After Pete King struck a reciprocity deal between U.S. and UK musicians' unions, The Tubby Hayes Quartet played the Half Note Club in New York and famed American tenor saxophonist Zoot Sims performed a four-week residency at Ronnie Scott's in November 1961. It was a first-ever engagement of prominent American musicians in a British club setting.

Eventually, Scott and King moved the club to its current location in 1965, with strong community support. Amidst all of their financial squeezes and crises, they marveled that they had never been approached for protection

---

[8] Kynaston, David. *Modernity Britain: Book Two: A Shake of the Dice, 1959-62.* Bloomsbury Publishing. Pg. 8.
[9] Kynaston, Ibid.

money by Soho racketeers.

> *The only contact we ever had with the underworld - well, as far as we know anyway - was when we were looking for new premises in the Gerrard Street days and a couple of heavies came in one night and said they would pass the word on. Lo and behold a couple of nights later we got a call and one of the Krays walked in and took us off to have a look at a club premises in Knightsbridge, Esmeralda's Barn. But it wasn't suitable. – Pete King* [10]

The Hickory House and Billy Taylor

GRUBER: What was a typical day like when you were in the Army Band?

COBHAM: In the mornings, it was really beautiful, I was so blessed, I lived with my mom in Jamaica, Queens, 129th Avenue off Rockaway Boulevard, nearby Kennedy Airport. The army was paying me 20 bucks a day to not stay on the post. That was the Military Ocean Terminal Brooklyn. Couldn't be more than five miles away from the Verrazano-Narrows Bridge. Fort Hamilton was around the bend, Sheepshead Bay. We sent off the guys to Vietnam or Germany by military ships about twice a week.

GRUBER: How did you get in, did you sign up and say, "I want to be in the band?"

COBHAM: Yes, you had to take an audition. I wanted to work in the Air Force band as I thought I would get to work with better musicians. I wasn't opposed to leaving town. They had a marching band, drum and bugle corps, that was called The Airmen of Note. Amazing, they played *Tattoos* opposite the (British) Grenadier Guards, and they would just blow everybody away with their unique marching drills and music style. They had an enclave in the middle of the USA.

GRUBER: Where there are not as many music alternatives for audiences.

COBHAM: They may play New York or Los Angeles, and no one would even notice. Generally, they are known for playing the fly-over states like

---

[10] Henrybebop.co.uk/frithst.htm

Nebraska. So, I said I wanted to enlist but the enlistment representatives couldn't guarantee I could get into the Air Force band. I had to trust my gut, I didn't believe these guys. I definitely didn't want to go to the Navy.

GRUBER: Was there a draft at that time?

COBHAM: Yes, sir, Vietnam. My number was up. I took a test when I went into the army, went to the MOTB band in Brooklyn, they gave me a clean bill of health, 'yeah, this guy can help us.' I never got that from the Air Force. I did basic training and I went to where the United States Army Field Band was. I had a shot at getting into the Field Band, which would have opened up doors for more ceremonial work, but they wanted cats who would be lifers. They would be investing a lot.

GRUBER: After basic training, you went right into the band?

COBHAM: You bet. They sent me to the U.S. Military School of Music, originally called the United States Naval School of Music, in Scope, Norfolk, Virginia. That's where I met Grover Washington, Cecil Bridgewater, John Charles. Grover went to the 19th Army Band, I think. Cecil went to the 172nd...

GRUBER: You have an incredible memory.

COBHAM: Cecil was married to a great jazz singer (Dee Dee Bridgewater). John and I ended up in MOTB, it was rockin'. Because I could live off-post, and I could moonlight.

GRUBER: I don't understand why they wanted you to live off-post.

COBHAM: I think they knew they were going to close it down. We weren't working every day.

GRUBER: Pretty good gig if you are going to be in the army, living at home with your Mom. Damn!

COBHAM: And for me it was perfect. Grady Tate was having a problem with his back and I ended up subbing for Grady with Billy Taylor when I could squeak in a weekend. We had a guy, CQ, Company Quarterly, had to stay open all the time, a guy named Tadje, clarinet player in the band. When everyone was off-post, he would sign them in to say they were on-post and of course we would pay him for it. He had to earn a living! He was from Iowa and the price was right. A couple of bucks. As a Spec 4, I was making $122 a month but for five dollars, I could make $700 working for Billy at a college date.

GRUBER: Big money at that time.

COBHAM: Man, when I looked in the envelope, I thought, it must be all ones (*laughter*).

GRUBER: Were you playing with Taylor every night?

COBHAM: At the Hickory House, yeah, every night, six nights a week.

GRUBER: Can you describe it?

COBHAM: Yeah, it was a steak house. Downtown in the meatpacking district, there was a place, The Old Homestead. Sculpture of a big old steer on the outside, where you could eat huge steaks, we're talking 15 ounces of meat on the bone. The Hickory House was like that. I would have it once a month. I couldn't afford it otherwise. But working with Billy? I loved working so much, I don't even know how much I got paid. Every night we got something to eat. But once a month you could order anything you wanted. It was a trio: piano, bass and small drum set, and we played behind the bar, amongst the liquor bottles, man, in essence. Most venues with jazz trios, they always played on this island in the middle.

GRUBER: Did you used to hang out on 52nd Street to listen to jazz?

COBHAM: No, I was busy, I was just trying to get in and out.

GRUBER: By that time, 'The Street' was in decline.

COBHAM: It was beyond decline, man. Some of those clubs, The Red Parrot, were still around. I was in the army; I was so paranoid that I would miss my reveille.

Dr. Billy Taylor (was) kind of a model. He made his connections. He was on *Sunday Morning*, CBS, well done show, people like Cronkite on it. He would do a segment from time to time, towards the end, a commentary on the arts. Oscar Peterson would come out. The people on that show were his biggest fans, used to hang out at clubs and listen to Billy. Part of that scene for a blink of the eye, I saw that and said, this is where I want to be.

Not generally publicized, but when you are playing venues like Radcliffe or Smith or Wellesley, Harvard, just in a small lounge, the receptions are attended by the intelligentsia. As a Spec 4 in the army, which is like a corporal, I was making $168 dollars a month; with Billy, I would come home with $700 for the night. Not just the money, it was the acceptance of the people who heard me and remembered me.

And he was teaching everywhere. The last time I was in his presence was at a presentation at the UNESCO headquarters in Paris. Those were the only kind of gigs that he did, and I loved it. When I first played with him, the Hickory House was the last jazz club on 52nd Street. We had a great time. That was school for me. On a couple of occasions, I darn near died trying to get back to the army base because we didn't finish until three o'clock in the morning; we started at 8 o'clock. That was 1966-67. My luck ran out and I got caught not being able to make a gig and he had to work without me and he never called me again. He had all these people. Ben Tucker, a bassist who was also a publicist and owned the rights to a tune called *Sunny*. There is a sub-stratum of artists and musicians who quietly do their thing and survive. They don't have to worry about the management apparatus that runs the music business.

GRUBER: 52nd Street, wasn't that where people would go after their gigs and jam all night?

COBHAM: After hours, people would be looking for a different environment to release themselves from and would play until the wee hours of the morning. They would get something to eat, find a place to stay overnight in Harlem or in New Jersey.

The Jazz Head: A Lunchtime Chat with Ronnie Scott's Paul Pace

Ronnie Scott's Managing Director Simon Cooke tells me there is one guy who best understands the DNA of the club, which acts are booked, what the venue tries to achieve musically and that's Paul Pace. After settling in to our seats in front of the empty bandstand late Thursday morning, Paul offers, "I'm the jazz head in the club, people come to me for the history. I am involved on an emotional level as a fan." I ask how he got involved with the club and why.

PACE: I came here as a schoolboy in '72. My first visit, I came up with some friends, we came up too late, we didn't book ahead, it was Sonny Rollins returning after his sabbatical. *Horn Culture* came out about that time. He was playing at Ronnie's with Rufus Harley on bagpipes, it was an interesting band. Didn't get in but (later) saw Zoot Sims, then Oscar Peterson, Buddy Rich. I studied architecture in the seventies…

GRUBER: Perfect preparation for working for a jazz club.

PACE: Certainly is! I used to come here very often. I used to see those posters around town and they were very good, strong graphics actually. There was this chunky font from the late sixties, worked very well for posters. In those days, a student membership was something like 40 pounds for a year and you got in for three pounds Monday through Thursday to see these amazing musicians.

GRUBER: At that time, what did the Ronnie Scott's brand mean to you, what were you expecting?

PACE: These were artists I had worshipped in records; to see them at close quarters was amazing. Coming into the room was just extraordinary, it was magical. We have retained most of the magic in the room by not changing it too much, the atmosphere created, the décor, the lighting, the sound was always good. Ronnie Scott would come into the room and if the sound was not quite the way he liked it, he would try to sort it out. You walked through that door and you were in jazz heaven. And I was madly in love with jazz. I was a little strange, my contemporaries were into progressive rock, Led Zeppelin and all the rest of it.

GRUBER: There are some that see an overlap there, as an aesthetic, as an aspiration, between progressive rock and jazz-rock fusion. Were there common threads there musically or in terms of intention?

PACE: Yes, there were because the virtuosity garnered in the straight-ahead jazz field was something that put these players in good stead, the likes of

Randy Brecker and Larry Coryell had fantastic jazz chops, were able to take, coming up through the rock era, and assimilate it into something else, into their own music. Although I went to a lot of iconic jazz people at Ronnie Scott's, I went to Billy Cobham, in Croydon for the first time, a gig in the Greyhound, around '73, at the time of *Spectrum*. Rock bands and horns: that made my connection to my contemporaries. I could rave about it to them and drummers could appreciate Billy Cobham's drum skills. Just before that Mahavishnu had been on TV on the BBC. All these forms were re-energizing both jazz and rock and I loved it. As much as I liked the swinging stuff, it was very exciting. And to be there when it was being created was quite something.

GRUBER: As you decide to book Bill year after year, what does his brand, his music mean to you?

PACE: I would hazard a guess that he is the most admired drummer after Buddy Rich. He's taken the art of playing drums to another level and he has kept the bar very high. He's been in the center of this jazz-rock fusion movement, from Dreams, Miles Davis, to *Mahavishnu* and his own bands, and he has fused a lot of different cultures from West Indian to jazz to classical. He has been a very progressive musician and has not looked back too much, he has been pushing forward.

GRUBER: Does the term fusion still mean anything to you? Particularly with Guy Barker's arrangements which are pretty hardcore big band.

PACE: It's still used. We use it in our music meetings. Scott Henderson, Mike Stern who is more jazz fusion, we make a distinction with rock fusion which is virtuosic, not as much improvisation, has more of a rock aesthetic. Fusion is certainly a style which has consolidated. When you mention fusion, people think of guitar-led thing, usually quite loud, many notes, rock rhythms.

GRUBER: What kind of experience do people come to Ronnie Scott's for these days?

PACE: There is a certain proportion of people who do come just because it's Ronnie Scott's. You can't actually rely on them. The competition is so fierce for people to use their leisure time. It is mostly artist-led. These shows are sold out because it's Billy Cobham. Guy Barker is certainly highly admired and it's a very exciting combination. Over the weekend you might get the tourist brigade, or people coming in for a party from outside London to go to Ronnie Scott's.

GRUBER: What is the club's place in the UK music scene?

PACE: It's the place where people want to play, whether it be jazz or other genres. We do try to keep the core of what Ronnie Scott's is about stylistically. It's kept the standards high. People recognize that and they would like a little bit of the stardust on them. If they're not that well known, they play at Ronnie's and it gives them a brand, and it goes on their CV. Even those who play upstairs will do their very best to tell people they played at Ronnie Scott's. It is a special brand and we protect the brand.

GRUBER: You booked Bill for the last 11 years.

PACE: Yes, since 2006. His first visit was 1968 with Horace Silver and Bennie Maupin. The other time he played here was Johnny Griffin's last performance here. Billy was on drums on a small kit.

GRUBER: How often does that happen, 11 consecutive years?

PACE: Georgie Fame does a week every year. Out of instrumentalists, it's quite rare.

GRUBER: What are they expecting when they come to see Billy? Why do you book him?

PACE: People who have grown up with his music, Mahavishnu and his own band, and they bring their friends and then you've got drum heads coming as well.

GRUBER: Who was Ronnie Scott?

PACE: Ronnie Scott was a saxophonist who came up with the big bands in this country, played with Ted Heath, and famously had a lengthy span with Pete King, then with Tubby Hayes and the Jazz Couriers; gave up the saxophone in order to run the business of Ronnie Scott's on Gerrard Street in 1959, then came over here in '65. And then three years later, Horace

Silver comes here with Billy Cobham. Ronnie Scott was a hard man to get to know. I had a few words conversation with him. He kept his own counsel. He had his close friends and he was much admired, a fantastic player. I saw the quintet many times. Very self-deprecating and his humor was along those lines. Incredible timing. He could tell the same jokes every night, near enough and everybody would laugh.

"Our next guest is one of the finest musicians in the country. In the city, he's crap."
– Ronnie Scott

GRUBER: Were you a fan of Mahavishnu back in the day?

PACE: I was. When I bought *Birds of Fire*, I remember being absolutely knocked out. I was finding it hard to take, there was so much happening (*laughs*). I admired it more than I enjoyed it. There was a lot of sophistication that I wasn't picking up on. Billy Cobham was my first foray into that era of music. With *Spectrum*, I related to it more because of the horns in the band. I was late teens, Blood, Sweat and Tears and Chicago, those bands had horn sections at that time, I enjoyed that music.

GRUBER: Any final thoughts about Bill's history, his music, his unique style?

PACE: Like all the great players, he is identifiable, he has developed his own concept. He has been the engine room of so many great bands. He himself is a shining example of a progressive and inventive musician and person. He was here with some children from the local school. You know yourself, he is a very warm person. (Pauses) He doesn't stand for any nonsense. I've been at the sharp end of his email about drum kit hire and transportation because we are on the front line. An inventive and extraordinary musician and a terrific band leader. His bands are always excellent. Aside of that, he rehearses his own band every day of the week. That's before the evening show. And that's rare. Most bands come in, do a sound check, a bit of rehearsal, some topping and tailing, then they do the evening show. When he's got his own band, he will run through the stuff and make sure it's absolutely spot-on.

GRUBER: In London, who is Guy Barker?

PACE: He is the go-to guy for arranging now but he is also regarded as one of the top trumpet players. Emerged from the ranks of the National Youth Jazz Orchestra in his teens and at that point he was a soloist of note; then he was picked up by Georgie Fame. Now he is arranging; *Amadeus* was extraordinary. He does a vocal special at London Jazz Festival; does the arrangements for the singers, the likes of Dee Dee Bridgewater and Kurt Elling. He has very good relationships with singers. He is a very approachable man, very nice to deal with and he has made so many good connections. There is an audience for him as well. If he plays with his own band here, we will sell the tickets.

The Corner Barbershop and the Grand Opera House

GRUBER: Your first show at Ronnie Scott's was with Horace Silver in 1968, three years after the move to the Frith Street location. Any memories from that show?

COBHAM: Yeah. The audience. Quincy Jones, Art Blakey, it was a George Wein tour. I think Mary Lou Williams, Chick Corea, McLaughlin were coming in and out because Ronnie's was like the corner barbershop for musicians, like the Professional Percussion Center (Eighth Avenue and Fifth Street, New York City) where you got your stuff fixed. You come in (at PPC) at 10 in the morning and standing by the door is Papa Jo Jones waiting to get in with a newspaper under his arm.

> *PAPA JO: You're late!*
>
> *COBHAM: Late for what?*
>
> *PAPA JO: I need to get a coffee.*
>
> COBHAM: *What??*

COBHAM: He opens the door and goes in and gets a coffee, says, "OK, what are we doing today?" He's not doing *anything*. He just sits there until it's time for him to play that night and just rattles on about this, that and the other thing. Then Buddy Rich would come in and say, "Jo, we said we were going to do this thing, you're teaching me for an hour."

PAPA JO: *How much money you got??*

And then they would just go upstairs and practice. You would hear all these different lines coming through.

GRUBER: So, he was a teacher.

COBHAM: Papa Jo was a teacher. He played with Teddy Wilson. He played with Benny Goodman. He played with Basie. If you can imagine, back then, 1968, '69, '70, to make a living, I was teaching there with Tony Williams, Max Roach, Elvin Jones, Papa Jo. Five of us had rooms. Frank Ippolito's.

Throughout the week, I ask members of the band and concertgoers about Ronnie Scott's place in the music world.

STEVE HAMILTON, keyboards: It's a bit of a jazz mecca this place. When I first moved to London, I was 20, 22 years old. You made it if you played at Ronnie Scott's and a lot of musicians think that to this day. You need to earn your stripes, get peer acceptance over a period of time to play here. It's always been a bit of a benchmark. The first few times I got to play here were in the support band in the '90s when Ronnie was still here. He was really cool, I got on really well with him. He used to come out and tell dry, funny jokes when he was introducing the bands. He was into chess and so was I, so we talked about it, pretty nerdy. I've played here many, many times. I've been living up in Scotland a long time so would come down for projects but, since playing with Bill, we play every year and I love coming here.

MIKE HOBART, *The Financial Times:* Ronnie's is the grand opera house of jazz. Going for 50 years, I think, against all the odds. I went in the early '60s. Jazz is a big church, soul, funk but Ronnie's has a hard jazz policy. It's the place, when you meet someone who plays sax, you ask, have you played at Ronnie Scott's?

Whereupon Ronnie Scott Tells Michael Watt to Fuck Off

During Thursday night's show, I am perched once again at the club bar. No complaints, I get to watch people come and go, the efficiency of the seating process, the nuances of each new performance and the different ways each new audience reacts to the band. Tonight, Paul Pace comes by to say hello, and walks me over to co-owner Michael Watt's table. A master of hospitality and storytelling, Michael ensures I am well-fed and watered; it's only with supreme discipline that I begin to decline refills of the table's very impressive champagne. As we chat during breaks in the performance (and some more in a follow-up call over Skype), I am curious how Michael met Ronnie and why he chose to become involved with the club.

MICHAEL WATT: In June of 1960, I got off a ship from New Zealand with a bunch of duty-free cigarettes to sell in London. I went to the Mandrake Club in Soho and they said go 'round and see Ronnie Scott. So, I went 'round there and he told me to fuck off.

I went back to the same club and they called him up and said, "Don't be a prick," buy these cigarettes. I had about twelve cartons of Marlboro. He offered us a deal which we accepted: two free nights in the club, two beers per night. No food. We tried to go back the third night. He caught us and told us to fuck off. And rumor has it, when he told us to piss off, I told him, one of these days I'll come back and buy the place. I don't remember saying that, but somebody told me that that actually happened. That was the old club in 1960. They moved to the new club in '65. I spent many, many nights there, both with money and without money. It was a sort of acceptable den of iniquity because when I had money I used to backhand the guys on the door to get in to get good seats. When I didn't have money, it was very difficult unless it was empty. That went on for years. At times, I flirted with him about buying the club when they kept running out of money to pay their VAT and tax bills. Went backwards and forwards for years.

When we did have money, we used to go to the downstairs bar and camp down there with musicians and drink copious quantities of champagne. And when we ran out, we used to go around the corner to Annabelle's and get some out the back door there. A lot of things went on there. It was a watering hole for all sorts of nondescript people. And that went backwards and forwards until Sally Greene, who I was in business with on a show called *Billy Elliott,* said to me, "If we can get our hands on Ronnie Scott's, do you want to partner?" So, I said, OK, let's give it a try. I said, you do the negotiations, I'll be at the back because I was sick and tired of wheeling and dealing with those guys, although Ronnie by then of course was long dead.

Sally Greene funded and engineered the refurbishment at the historic Old Vic theatre after acquiring it in 1998. The million-pound (some estimates are double) investment she and partners made in upgrading Ronnie Scott's using famed Parisian designer Jacques Garcia generated big excitement and anticipation among London jazzers and also some ribbing from the press.

> *For those anoraks who believe that jazz can only be truly appreciated in louche, poorly lit dives, the good news is that the club has retained its trademark brothel-red table lighting. Getting in is much easier now that you won't have to fight through a crush of bodies queuing at the bar, which has been sensibly moved from the side next to the entrance to the middle at the back. The carpet upon which oceans of drinks have spilled down the years and on to which the great jazz trumpeter Dizzy Gillespie once threw up has finally been replaced.* [11]

GRUBER: Running a jazz club is a difficult business and you're a tough, smart successful business person. What did you see in the club – outside of nostalgia, affection and a love for music – that you thought was sustainable over time as a successful business?

WATT: Yeah, that's certainly a decent question. The fact of the matter was that the place had been run on a very bad business basis and even when Pete King took over, and he was a bit of a businessman with money, they still ran it on a sort of a piecemeal basis. If they had a house and picked up a lot of money, then they would start looking to book another act down the line. It wasn't run like a business.

They made one mistake big time: they didn't realize that the brand was iconic. They did not take advantage of the brand. When we got our hands on it, we said, this could be a rough ride for the first couple of years, but the brand is so big, and with London short of watering holes like this, we should give it a go. It was a gamble. We had a series of problems with managers. We had managers that spent most of the time drinking the grog,

---

[11] Sandall, Robert. "Ronnie Scott's Says Goodbye Sticky Carpets - Hello Decent Food and Air Conditioning." *Daily Telegraph.* June 24, 2016.

we had managers down there trying to fuck all of the waitresses, until Cooke arrived and he was a much more sensible choice. He got the place shaped up. Having cleaned it up, spruced it up, some of the guys in the press took a shot at us saying we were turning it into a gin palace, which my partner sort of had a mind to do, but she quickly backed out in what was our only argument since. Debate's a better word. The partnership has never had one fallout since those early months in the entire 13 years. That helps when everybody is in a balanced zen mode to run a place. It's a happy operation, the staff are very good. We've taken advantage of the iconic name, and people come near and far and the bands we book are considered to be some of the best in the world.

> *When Pete King and I decided to open a jazz club in 1959, I took heart from the fact that we were starting with two significant advantages. First of all, we knew that we couldn't lose money in the venture because we didn't have any; and secondly, we didn't know that running a jazz club was impossible. In the early days, people would say to us, "Surely there must be easier ways of earning a living?" And of course we would reply, "Who's earning a living?" – Ronnie Scott* [12]

GRUBER: What unique place in the urban life of Londoners does Ronnie Scott's hold?

WATT: Well. It's big time. It's a destination. The fact that the place is always sold out gives an idea of how popular it is.

GRUBER: You've been booking Billy Cobham there for the last 11 years. It's fairly unusual. What motivates you to want to bring him back?

WATT: He sells out. Second is that he is considered to be one of the great all-time drummers. From the point of view of Ronnie Scott's audience and indeed from audiences anywhere in the world. And he has got a charisma about him which makes people want to come see him.

GRUBER: Why is bringing music to kids important to you?

WATT: My background is working illegally in America in the '60s, all linked to jazz. If I made any money, I would spend it at the Metropole Café on

---

[12] Henrybebop.co.uk/frithst.htm

Times Square or anywhere else I could find. Hal Ramsay's Lighthouse on the West Coast. I grew up with this kind of music, greatly influenced by Baker and Mulligan and Miles Davis. And then later on, of course, Bill Evans.

Kids, when they participate in something musical, find it quite contagious and their everyday concerns just go out the window. As a further benefit, they think, that was great, I want to participate, I want to learn an instrument. It's a great buzz for a kid. You could see the joy they are having. And they are all like that. Billy Cobham does his thing with kids. They never forget it.

GRUBER: Did you spend a lot of time personally with Ronnie Scott? Who was he and what motivated him to build this legacy?

WATT: He was a paradoxical character. A lot of the time I spent with him (*laughs*) was quite spikey. We used to misbehave in there. A lot of booze, it's a hard thing to describe. I had a better relationship with a lot of people than I had with him. But, when people asked why he was running the place so bad, he said, I am a musician, I am not really a club owner. I don't have the skills or business discipline, I am only here for the music, and any money I have, I will pour it into the acts. Of course, he poured it into bookmakers and others. Everybody has a glowing story but he could be a difficult gentleman.

Ronnie Scott commenting on the early days on his club's cuisine, "A thousand flies can't be wrong."

GRUBER: What music are you listening to these days?

WATT: Hahaha, if I told you... I'm listening to choral music from a group called The Sixteen, which is baroque, a slightly out-there electronic act called Biosphere, I'm listening to Simon Philips, to a trumpeter out of New Orleans, a young hipster, I'm going to get the name to you. There is so much to listen to you, I've got over 6,000 iTunes files. Keely Smith, since I saw her in Las Vegas when I worked there. I always listen to Stanley Clarke. John Beasley is a personal friend; I listen to him. Anything that Vince Mendoza comes out with, some far out stuff like Ralph Flanagan's old stuff. Difficult to tell you exactly.

GRUBER: That's a pretty good list.

The Move to Europe

Bill is first introduced to Europe at his Ronnie Scott's gig with Horace Slver in 1968, then is back several times, including the epic 1977 all-star jam with Stan Getz et al in Montreux, Switzerland. I'm curious what drove him to move to Switzerland in 1980, where he resides to this day.

COBHAM: Curiosity started it. I took it personally that I could not negotiate the streets logically in the city of Zurich. I wanted to just hang here and learn all about Europe in six weeks. Looked in a newspaper, the *Herald Tribune*, small apartment column next to obituaries. Saw three apartments, one in Zurich. In an American accent, guy picked up the phone, can I help you? My name is Cobham, calling about the rental. Cobham? I know a musician named Cobham. Really? You want to rent the apartment; you play drums? This is amazing, he says, I'm a drummer too. Had all my stuff sent over from San Francisco, old Hamburg Steinway which we still have here.

GRUBER: What was your experience with race there?

COBHAM: Six weeks later on a Sunday, a knock on the door, a guy who says he came to check on the oil and the heat in the building, I knew it was police. Invited him in, all in black like some kind of a ninja. "Why are you here? I think you are not here to check the oil. Talk to me, what do you want to know." He asked questions. A week or two later a policeman came and asked me to come down to the local precinct. They knew I left a wallet on top of a car in the snow and nobody touched it. I had signed an agreement that I couldn't get out of for six months. It was exactly correct for me to be there, like some kind of mystical move. I am not that social. I was just looking for peace and quiet. The Swiss thought that if they ignored me I would go away. But I stayed.

The Swiss believe you are trying to take something from them. It's subdued, it's in the body language. If you decide to go into Le Ambassador, where watches are sold, and you appear to be of a social community below what should be in the store, you might have a problem. A man might say, "Can I help you?" "I'm not quite sure. *Can you?*" Oprah walked into a store on (elite Zurich shopping street) Bahnhofstrasse in flip-flops and her hair in a kerchief to see a bag on the top, 45,000 francs. International incident. You don't bring that here.

GRUBER: Many black American artists from Josephine Baker and Dexter Gordon to Richard Wright and James Baldwin relocated to western Europe because they thought there was greater artistic and social freedom. You didn't leave the United States to go to Europe because of race.

COBHAM: I left because of work. I left because of the concept of what I was doing and playing. No, my decision had a lot to do with why other black musicians went to Europe to work, because of what was going on in the United States at the end of the '70s, when you had a major disco thing. I knew that wasn't me, sit around and compete with people who wanted to be chameleons. Most musicians, rather than work on the art of being a good musician, they look at trends. They want to get in with whoever it is who is controlling the scene because they want to work.

GRUBER: So, you are saying we never got close to the Billy Cobham disco era.

COBHAM: No. As a matter of fact, it might even be on iTunes, *B.C.* was a co-production with the late Wayne Henderson, who played trombone with the Jazz Crusaders. Sold the least of any record I made with a major company. It was all pre-smooth jazz. He wanted to do this disco thing with me. Columbia wanted to do it too to sell more records which was of course logical. *B.C.* was my only attempt at the disco platform and not a direction I felt comfortable working in.

GRUBER: Chet Baker at around that same time talked about his inability to get work in the United States even though he was quite popular.

COBHAM: But Brian, it's quite different. Chet was in Amsterdam. I met him. Mike Stern was in his band at the time. It was a whole other world. They stayed close to home which was at the Paradiso on Milky Way, where the opium dens were. Stern was trying to come out of that stuff. He was on the road with me with Michael Urbaniak, Tim Landers and Gil Goldstein,

Glass Menagerie band. Chet and I were both Dodger freaks so we would chat.

GRUBER: Did your Panamanian background cause you to see race differently?

COBHAM: It's not about the discrepancy between white and black, it is more the discrepancy between black and black. You have the American black, African-American, and then you have the others who hail from places like Jamaica, Brazil, Africa itself. Africans born in Africa are probably treated better by Afro-Americans than Caribbean blacks who have emigrated to places like Florida after the fact.

It's been very difficult for me to have anyone in the black community to hire me for anything. I have never been on BET (Black Entertainment Television) in my life. George Duke lived there. He and Stanley Clarke launched their acts off of BET. I wouldn't even know where to find it. Very difficult for me to find my music at any time on a black radio station. I can certainly use the help of any promotional organization. There was a lot of intra-racial tension within the black community, and nothing new, by the way. It's cool by me. It is simply an aspect of the Achilles heel of the human race. I don't take it as a monkey on my back. Read General Colin Powell's book, Jamaican family man. There were some (Caribbean) blacks who were involved in the movement, like Harry Belafonte.

GRUBER: Did you look up to Belafonte at that time?

COBHAM: No, in the sixties, I was a high school kid, going in the military. Racism but in a different way. For me, I could see things happening. I decided to focus on what I did best to avoid that. That was, to play my ass off and make a point of using my abilities to open doors. It was good because I avoided a lot of the pitfalls that a lot of musicians fall into, which was a road of mediocrity. Where everybody is doing what everybody else is doing and somebody else is deciding for them where and what to do when. When it came time for me to work, I thought, I can't work in this country any more. The kind of music that I would like to play no longer has life. Because some marketing firm decided we should play *In the Navy*, because that's what they are pushing now.

I was on a mission. I knew what I wanted to do in life, I knew how I wanted to go about it, from when I was a kid. I wanted to be a good musician. I wanted to teach others based upon my personal experiences and how they related to the available historical information. Based on my facility to play, it told the truth. I worked at what I did and chose to share what I did.

Moscow's Le Club, the Blue Note Milano, and The Development

Ronnie Scott's is not the only iconic European jazz club to invite Bill back each year. New York's famed Blue Note selected Milan, Italy as the site for its European expansion. I worked with Blue Note Milano Managing Director Alessandro Cavalla on a livestreaming experiment some years back. I asked him by email why he keeps bringing Bill back.

> *Billy Cobham is one of the greatest musicians who have shaped the Blue Note Milano story since the opening of our club. We were pleasantly hit, the first time he played here, to see a star musician, like he is, showing up at the club entrance with his own van and starting down-loading his drum kit. And every time he comes back, he is still very active in the process of setting up his instrument and the show in general.*
>
> *Billy Cobham's concert is a favorite among Blue Note's audience, who appreciates its quality, 'spectacularity' and virtuosity, and is on the billboard for several days each year, always in demand. We are honored to share a small part of the path of an extraordinary artist, one of jazz fusion's capital artists, capable of inventing a unique sound and style of his own.*

One other top shelf saxophonist decided he ought to be in the club business. Igor Butman built Le Club into the best jazz destination in Moscow and one of *Downbeat's* "Top100 Jazz Venues of the World." After launching in 1998, he pressed his manager to bring in more big names. She was sensitive to the ego of artists and managers. Before landing and staging Bill's show, she had an intense experience with one artist. So, she decided she would avoid talking to Bill if at all possible. And she had "a kind of rule, not to be involved with any musicians" who were coming to perform. "Every night Billy was hungry," she recalls, not surprising after the brutal caloric release of a Cobham power-drumming performance, "asking for apple pie or asking Igor to take him to a 24-hour diner." But, each time, Igor asks his manager to go with them. After a few days of this, Bill asks her if they could have coffee in the morning. They meet the next day and, after talking about a project, Bill asks, "Now, tell me about Faina." She answers, simply, "A single woman, working 24 hours a day, I have a son." On the way to the airport, Bill asks her to keep a snare drum for him. She asks, reasonably, how he planned to get it back. Bill answers, you will come visit to Switzerland.

FAINA COBHAM: Then we were talking on the phone, beginning of 2000 (Bill had performed in December 1999). In February, Bill came to play again at the request of Igor. This time, he asked, would you like to go with me to Panama. And I am looking at him again, *of course, I want to go* and he said, "OK, we will go together." Then he started to come back more and more. I went to Italy with him. He was at first introducing me as, "This is Faina, she is Kazakh." I'm not Kazakh! I'm from Kazakhstan, but not Kazakh. Then a few months later, he said, this is my girlfriend. *Ah, a development.* Then five years later I became his wife.

I ask Faina what drives Bill to continue to create and perform.

FAINA: It is his life. I am still surprised, trying to imagine how it happens, where is it coming from, when he is writing this complex music. I hope over the years I have become a person who inspires him. It's beautiful. A lot of people ask, do you understand who Billy is, that he is a big artist, and I say, yes, I understand, but the main thing for me is, he is my husband, a person who is very kind and respectful and I love him very much.

GRUBER: Was the Ronnie Scott's week unique? You have seen him in so many musical situations.

FAINA: I saw projects with big bands and even symphony orchestras. I was impressed with Guy Barker that he could make arrangements, for example, with *Sal Si Puedes*. For me, that, with a big band, sounds more impressive and exciting than with a small group. Every day the quality improved. In the beginning, I didn't think it would be better than hr Bigband (Hessischer Rundfunk is the public broadcaster for the German state of Hesse), but as the week went on, it was kind of, wow, that's it.

GRUBER: Guy talked about the hr Bigband. Tell me about the history of how that came about.

FAINA: Started with a project of Mahavishnu Orchestra arrangements, *Meeting of the Spirits*. Bill was invited to come and play with their arrangements of 10 compositions. It was wonderful. I loved the project and then we performed in Australia with a 100-piece symphony orchestra, 50 violins playing the guitar parts.

GRUBER: When did you start to manage his business affairs?

FAINA: When I moved to Switzerland, it was not easy for Billy or for me. He was used to working alone, controlling everything. Then I started piece by piece, taking from him, I can do this, can I do this. When Billy felt comfortable that I can manage something, I would do it. It took a few years. Billy has the last word; I am kind of an advisor. To me, I was buying art, now I am selling art, so I can understand the mentality of the buyer.

GRUBER: From your experience from the buyer's side, what do you think people are coming to see?

FAINA: They have a history, they know Billy as Mahavishnu and *Spectrum*, and people who come to the concerts want to hear old tunes, still. When I met Billy, he was tired to play *Stratus* but people would be upset if he didn't do one or two of those tunes. They were listening and waiting.

GRUBER: People are paying good money and have some emotional investment in these tunes. Bill's music affected so many people, even many of the musicians in the show. What is the right mix?

FAINA: It's how he feels in a night. Sometimes I fight with him, but it doesn't work. People are trying to understand the new material, to mix with *Stratus*. After the shows, a lot of people are asking for the new CDs. Different generations come, his generation and then their kids come along and it's very nice. A lot of kids like this music. My sister has a grandson, Michael, in Argentina, who came to the concert, 10 years old. After the concert, he asked my sister to play Billy's CD every day.

I finish my talk with Faina on Skype when the two are safely back in

Schupfen, in the canton of Bern, Switzerland. Bill pops in and out of the conversation while making the two of them French toast, which he insists is very, very good. I ask him, what are the benefits or downsides of having a wife as a business manager?

BILLY COBHAM: It depends on who the person is. We are a team. I do not rule; we develop a consensus on which way to go. You can't let an artist just do whatever they want. That's (the value of) having someone you are close to, "Are we in this, the good, bad and the ugly?" I asked Faina not to take on anybody else as manager. We do everything together, shopping, working on stuff, 70 percent of the time we don't agree but we figure out how things can work with the hand we were dealt. She has opinions, I have mine.

GRUBER: Bill seemed to enjoy his session with the Soho school kids.

FAINA: Billy enjoys working with kids and young musicians. They can carry his style and his school in the future. Beginners try to repeat exactly what he was doing. And some say, I can't play like Billy Cobham, why should I continue? We were in Kazakhstan, to meet my parents, and my girlfriend's friend was a drummer, then suddenly became a tailor. When he found out that Billy was having breakfast in my girlfriend's kitchen, he almost died, was in shock, he didn't believe her. Then we came to a club and he came and said when *Spectrum* and Mahavishnu became available in Kazakhstan, he stopped playing, and he said to Billy, "It happened because of you!"

Sometimes I am sorry that we met a little bit late to provide a small person who could be a student.

GRUBER: How have you and Bill adapted to the changes in the music business, both the recording side and the touring side?

FAINA: I know with CDs; distribution is almost zero. I don't even try to find distributors. We are the record company. We press CDs. We distribute after performances.

GRUBER: Have online services like Spotify and Pandora and iTunes replaced CD revenue?

FAINA: I am not involved in that, but people still want a record in their hands with a signature. We had an offer to do memory sticks, it is easy to transport but it is not an option. For me, I am a fan of records, CDs which you can open and touch and see the signature of your idol, your artist.

5 THE ART OF THE RHYTHM SECTION

I first noticed Mike Hobart opening night at the back of the club as he made notes for his *Financial Times* review. Mike's April 25, 2014 FT feature recognized Bill as "one of the few drummers to lead a band into the Billboard Top Fifty" with 1973's *Spectrum* release, noting that it led the industry publication's jazz album charts while scoring 26 in overall album sales. "To this day," he wrote, "no drummer matches his ability to blend rock power with funk groove, and jazz finesse with technical precision."

I tracked him down by phone Friday morning to get his reflections on why Londoners have been coming to Bill's shows at Ronnie's for 11 years.

HOBART: London is a very sophisticated city musically. There is a large core audience, certainly from the '70s when Billy Cobham was coming up, when his jazz-funk-fusion cross left a large impact. People are very aware of what he did musically. And you've got a new audience that just appreciates him as a great drummer.

GRUBER: What surprised or impressed you about Barker's arrangements, particularly of classic fusion tunes like *Stratus*?

HOBART: He got the essence of them. He reworked them to…what I really liked about it, it wasn't just a showcase for Billy as a soloist. He is a superb big band drummer. He got a balance between showcasing the big band and flourishes and trills and voicings on the one hand and presenting Billy

Cobham as a superb craftsman, who besides being a great artist is an unselfish drummer who can fit in with the big bands.

Red Baron was simply great. I thought (during the extended intro), *what is this, I know this...* It's a jam session favorite. You have to know the *Red Baron* when someone calls it out in a jam, whether you are in Argentina, anywhere in the world. Really good, Barker is a good guy, a good musician and arranger.

> *The encore, Red Baron, was a Cobham classic given an imaginative makeover by Barker. It opened with tricky interlocking brass, featured a slow burn from Hitchcock and peaked with a rumble of drums. The audience, mirroring Cobham, left beaming from ear to ear.* [13]

GRUBER: Were there observations or musings about the show that did not make their way into the review?

HOBART: The strength of the trombone section above all. Nigel (Hitchcock, alto sax) is Nigel and everyone else is good, but the trombonists were exceptional. Billy's drum solos...he has the reputation for being all about muscle, but that's completely wrong. Anyone who knows anything about music wouldn't say that. Huge technique, which he keeps in check most of the time. He has got a sound; it doesn't matter where he is, he could play on tin cans and a broomstick, it will still sound like Billy Cobham.

GRUBER: The audience responded with rousing ovations to the horn solos. I'm an American living on a Thai island, so I don't know these guys, but I assume the band members are recognizable, esteemed British jazz musicians.

HOBART: Most of them. Like most jazz musicians, they are also studio musicians, they do shows, all sorts of things. Excellent craftsmen.

GRUBER: And Guy Barker?

---

[13] Hobart, Mike. 'Billy Cobham with the Guy Barker Big Band, Ronnie Scott's, London - technically superb." *Financial Times.* June 13, 2017.

HOBART: Guy has become an esteemed figure. He has paid his dues for 30 years, worked really, really hard, has worked and worked and worked as an arranger and bandleader and has become a major figure in British jazz; imaginative, has his own style and very deep roots in the music, R &B, loads and loads of things.

I thank Mike for his time and, after remarking that a chat about Bill's legacy is a nice way to spend the morning, he adds:

"Bill helped transform how we conceive and convene the rhythm section. A lot of it comes from the drum. Until the drums change, nothing really changes. It is when the rhythm section changes that's when the whole thing changes."

> *Cobham had perfected a style of drumming that combined jazz fluency with rock power and the discipline of a seasoned studio session musician...and the thunderous rolls, fiendish riffs and brittle light-touch grooves became a template for jazz-rock fusion. ...Cobham, though, remains the power on the throne.* [14]

GRUBER: Where do you think Bill's place is in music history?

HOBART: Very few people can come up with Latin, swing, and make that change into funk. He really was able to make that transition. Maybe because he came up with Latin music, he's got that military thing going. He is a monster. He is up there with Max Roach and Elvin Jones. All revolutions are evolutions. He is a very big, substantial person in the jazz firmament. I spoke to him a couple of years ago. He is everything you expect a jazz musician to be. Articulate, thoughtful about the world, focused on art and craft. Art is always based on craft. He has both.

"An Extra Breath of Air:" A Conversation with Ron Carter

I first met Ron Carter backstage at New York's Blue Note, before a January 2013 show with Bill and saxophonist Donald Harrison Junior. The occasion

---

[14] Hobart, Mike. 'Billy Cobham's Spectrum 40, Ronnie Scott's, London – review," *Financial Times,* February 6, 2014.

was a performance of the music on Donald's *Heroes* record, featuring and honoring his musical heroes Cobham and Carter. Donald Harrison is the inspiration for two of the principal characters in HBO's *Treme* series, as well as being Big Chief of the Congo Nation Afro-New Orleans Cultural Group.

Even the casual jazz fan will have heard Ron Carter's name. He's appeared on over 2,000 recordings, the most-recorded jazz bassist ever. There's not much debate that he is the best in the world, Bill acknowledges that backstage, though both he and Ron resist the idea of grading or comparing musicians. While Ron flirted briefly with an electric bass, he is a diehard double-bassist, the large acoustic instrument also known as stand-up bass.

There are considered to be two great Miles Davis quintets. Ron was a member of the second, along with Herbie Hancock, Wayne Shorter, and Tony Williams. He joined in 1963, appearing on *Seven Steps to Heaven* and the follow-up *E.S.P.* Like Bill, he is a prolific sideman, playing with Freddie Hubbard, Lee Morgan, McCoy Tyner, Horace Silver, a who's who of jazz over the years. He was honored in 2010 with France's *Commander of the Ordre des Arts et des Lettres* and elected to the *Down Beat* Jazz Hall of Fame in 2012.

I called Ron for insights on his decades-long collaborations with Bill as bass-percussion partners. He was the generous, good-humored maestro seen on countless stages in every corner of the planet.

Carter met Cobham at a CTI recording date; they both performed in-studio for Creed Taylor's label. Ron thinks it may have been a Grover Washington session. Someone said, "There is a guy who just got out of the army, pretty good drummer, his name is Billy Cobham," and so they invited Bill to play the date.

Bill thinks it was in 1967 while still in the army.

> *I came to sub for a really special person named Freddie Waits. It was an honor to be asked, I was like a fledgling. It was wonderful to just be in the process with all of the guys, Ron included. I am looking at myself going, I can't imagine I am with these people; I shouldn't be here yet. It started out there.*
>
> *They browbeat me about things I needed to know right away, for all the right reasons. I hit the ground running. There were a lot of things that I didn't know. In those days, being involved in the recording industry as a studio musician, I thought*

that was going to be my life, coming out of the military. That is not so easy, you have to go through those schools of hard knocks. And I was prepared for that in my mind. It was about what I could learn from it. [15]

GRUBER: Do you recall your first impression of Bill?

CARTER: In a studio, there's not much of an impression. It's kind of already tuned for you, they are already set up for the recording. You want to see a guy in a different kind of environment. I heard him playing somewhere in town and I was pleased with how he tuned his drums in a live situation. I kind of judge how a guy plays or how I enjoy listening to him play by how he tunes the drums. Which allows the bass player an extra breath of air when the bass drum is tuned correctly and the snare drum is the correct brightness and the tom-toms are not tuned in between pitches and stuff like that. He is really aware of how the drum sound is so important to not just his sound but to the sound of the bass player and the band.

GRUBER: You played on *E.S.P.* Bill believes that was the first true jazz fusion album. Does the term fusion mean anything to you? Does it reflect anything important happening in music at that time?

CARTER: I'm not sure fusion is the best word, but it describes the mindset of some of those guys who were trying to combine the electronic stuff with the jazz community. In any event their presence and there not being so strong an industry left a lot of things for the jazz players to consider. Among them, trying to make sure that the sound in the club was always good. And two, when you had a good gig, making sure that the band sounds as good live as it sounds on the record. They brought that to the community of jazz, and I certainly appreciate that insistence that the sound be as near perfect as possible, rather than accepting it's a jazz club so it can't be all right.

GRUBER: Is that important to you, the venue that you play in, do you have some favorite clubs where you feel better performing, or once you are in your space that has the minimum physical requirements, does it not matter

---

[15] From Brian Gruber's backstage interview at the Blue Note in New York on January 9, 2013, with Billy Cobham, Ron Carter, and Donald Harrison Junior. youtu.be/CqEKo2zX0Rw

to you what club you are in?

CARTER: By and large it really doesn't matter. What I try to do, Brian, is to try to have the sound guys spend the whole week, spend the whole night. Club owners try to save money by having the sound guy do the opening night and maybe one night mid-week. In the meantime, the band sound changes, the band gets warmed up, they get more familiar with the room, the audience goes from a full house to a half a house, the piano needs to be retuned; so many factors that change after opening night that the band and the house need to have someone who can constantly monitor the sound as the band changes and as the room changes. Clubs now are starting to understand that's important not just to the band but to the customers who come, not just opening night, not just the opening set, but the second set of the third night or the last night. They want the band to sound good each night and they want that sound to represent just as good as what they hear in their homes. They realize that is important for their clientele.

GRUBER: When you do a week or several shows in a venue, do you have a process or an outlook as to how you want to use each of those days differently?

CARTER: Interesting. Last year, in Detroit, I worked four nights with four different groups, a nonet, big band, quartet, trio, presented four different views of the music. When I do one week at a club, say Catalina in California, I have a program I present to the band during the course of the sound check. An order of two sets if it's a two-set night. They are never guessing what the tune is for the night. Plan a story for two 75-minute sets; the band knows my process for the week. Our job, their job, my job is to develop the storyline. Think what they did not do right this night, because they have four chances to get it right for the next four nights.

GRUBER: You have an esteemed history of teaching in the academic world and in a variety of venues. Do you enjoy teaching?

CARTER: Absolutely.

GRUBER: What do you like about it?

CARTER: Watching students grow under my assistance, how the bass has a voice, how they can develop their own voice on this bass, how to maintain their instrument, how to pick the right strings, make the bass sound as you want it to sound, to understand how the bass sound works as a physicist, as a sound box, how hard to play the strings, where to play them, these kinds of details. I enjoy teaching them because most kids, no one stops to tells them. To have kids start with me in this process and watch them understand, which opens up other avenues for them, is quite a joy for me.

> *Any teacher who wants to teach has ideas they want to propagate to somebody else besides their grandmother. They want to have students that can take this idea, this propagandized view and develop it somewhere else. Secondly, teachers, a lot of them don't really have an understanding of how to teach, what to teach. I have that kind of skill level so I don't mind using it if I have the time.* [16]

GRUBER: Is there a unique Ron Carter approach to the instrument?

CARTER: You have to ask those kids!

GRUBER: What did you learn from Miles as a bandleader?

CARTER: *(Long pause)* How important tempo is. And how to trust the input of the guys who I am surrounding myself with. If you hired those guys, let them do what they do, you know? Watch what they do, listen to what they do, see how they develop an idea, how do they remember from night to night what didn't work and try to work on a better approach to this particular chord, or this particular tune, or this particular set of changes; to watch that take place and be responsible for some of that is a great thing to be a part of. One the great things about being a bandleader is that shared responsibility to get better every night.

> *Miles habitually walked offstage to let him solo. Coltrane, alone and under the spotlight, had to strengthen his language. Coltrane joked that Davis gave him little guidance. Responding to a question about whether Miles had specifically told him to play as far out as he could, Coltrane responded, "Miles? Tell me something? That's a good one!"* [17]

GRUBER: Did you spend much time with Miles offstage?

---

[16] Ibid, Blue Note interview with Ron Carter.
[17] Ratliff, Ben. *Coltrane: The Story of a Sound.* Farrar, Straus and Giroux. 2007. Kindle Edition, location 563.

CARTER: No, he lived in my neighborhood for a while on 77th Street. I would go by occasionally but we didn't really hang out much past the gigs.

GRUBER: Were you a fan of Mahavishnu Orchestra? Do you recall your initial impressions of their music?

CARTER: I am interested in any kind of music. With that specific band, the volume was so loud that the bass sounded like under audio-wise, didn't have the same kind of presence. I didn't appreciate that but I enjoyed listening to the music. Bill was a part of a wave of musicians in that era who made jazz fusion much more viable with his presence.

I mention Mahavishnu bassist Rick Laird's claim that his hearing was shot after performing in front of those massive speakers - and Bill's 38-inch gong - which draws a hearty laugh from Ron.

GRUBER: What motivated you to want to play and record with Bill over the years?

CARTER: Great drum sound; drums are pitched in the level of intonation that allows the bass range to be audible wherever I feel his notes. That's very important to me.

GRUBER: Do you have any favorite memories or stories about Bill on or off stage?

CARTER: When Bill plays with a trio, or quartet - me, Herbie and him, or Donald Harrison, him and I - he uses a smaller drum set. I admire him for realizing his normal kit is not necessary for this trio gig. Don't need that stuff for certain size ensembles. You can play just as well with one floor tom, one bass drum, only three cymbals. I admire him for understanding what his environment needs to make him be a part of that band.

GRUBER: Ron, what you are doing these days and what goals do you have for this stage of your career?

CARTER: I have a couple jazz classical records. My next hope is I can get some funds to do Bach motets. If I can find the budgetary possibility to hire eight singers, to replace the bass voice with the string bass, that's my current dream. Other than that, I am enjoying being 80 years old.

Backstage, a couple of hours before showtime, there is the setting of plates and silverware as the fellas shuffle in and out of the lounge, getting mentally ready for the evening's entertainment. Which often involves inane bullshitting. And tonight, for the first time, they will play two shows, not one.

ORR: This water is still, but it is not just still, it says it is 'delightfully still.'

MONDESIR: (Studying the label) It is actually delightfully still.

ORR: It's really fucking delightful.

BARKER: It's Friday night. I think last night was a rehearsal for tonight. Get the chops together, warmed up. I did sit down just before I went out and managed to get three bars in the cello concerto that should move it along and make me be inspired tomorrow, I hope.

ORR: I'm not really a composer but I write music just about every day. A friend of mine said, you should write every day as you practice every day.

BARKER: There is a great film composer called Gabriel Yared, a good friend of mine, who wrote the score for *The English Patient*. We worked together on *The Talented Mr. Ripley*. He insists you've got to write every day even if you have got no reason to write. Even if you have no project, it doesn't matter. It's understanding what the colors are. What instruments can really do. Balance acoustics.

ORR: Have you always had to balance between playing and composing?

BARKER: No. I was playing all the time, then composing, and writing took over and I was hardly playing at all. It was only the end of last year I was trying to play a bit more again.

I've seen Steve Hamilton perform numerous times with Bill. As with almost everyone I meet during my visit, he has a story of his first experience with Bill's music as a boy.

HAMILTON: I was seven years old. My dad had an extensive vinyl collection. Before I was old enough to listen to the music, I liked looking through them all, at the album covers. He had quite a few Billy records. I remember being intrigued by some of the covers and titles, like *Glass Menagerie*. I didn't know what a menagerie was (*laughter*) but it sounded incredibly exotic and the covers were quite psychedelic. Even at that age, I stumbled across the visual element of Billy's records. It wasn't until later that I actually heard the music.

GRUBER: Where does Bill sit in the jazz firmament for you, to use Mike Hobart's term?

HAMILTON: For me, he sits at the top. I cannot think of any drummer, living or dead, that can play all of the styles of music that Bill can play very comfortably. Usually guys get famous for doing one thing really, really well, but Bill does it all really, really well and he became famous because he had an element of physicality and creativity, he was able to do things on the drums that nobody thought possible. Latin, swing, funk, loud, soft, time signatures, he writes the music, he can go from a small kit to the biggest drum kit you've ever seen. Who can compare to this? And that's forgetting about what he does technically which is almost un-emulat-able.

GRUBER: How is this gig different from other gigs you've done with Bill? Yes, there are some horns, but what have you seen differently from Bill?

HAMILTON: He has had to put on more of the big band drummer hat. It's still 'drum-led' so there is an interesting balancing act going on between, 'am I the center of attention' or 'am I accompanying other musicians,' a lot of see-sawing, all at a very masterful level. I get to watch from a very close position, right next to the cymbals and toms. There is a lot more to it than anybody would ever understand.

GRUBER: For you, what's different, more rhythm responsibilities?

HAMILTON: A little less content to play than with a smaller band. We came into it thinking, we don't really know what this is going to sound like so let's make sure the quartet is really solid. I don't think Bill expected it to be as good as it is (*laughter*). These guys came in on the first rehearsal and that was it. It was already happening.

GRUBER: How long did everyone have the music for?

HAMILTON: I don't even know. I don't think some of those guys even looked at it before, that's what they do. They are well paid, they just come in and nail it.

GRUBER: You rehearsed as a rhythm section first.

HAMILTON: The reason is we have played with Bill collectively for many years so we know these tunes. It's actually sometimes harder to play something you've played before, now with a couple of extra bars here and an extra section, so if you are not careful you just go on autopilot. Bill quickly got to the point where he was not even looking at the music. He is very fast, soaking it up like a sponge, so he is already off the charts for most of the gig.

GRUBER: As a music fan, what was your experience watching the horn section, and watching the solos, the relationship of the players with Guy and Bill?

HAMILTON: Typically, in a big band you have guys good at one thing, not so good at other things. It's unusual to have a situation where every guy in the band is also a ridiculously good soloist. Guy handpicked the lineup for this gig because he knew the music was going to be very challenging. And he knew he could write certain things in the arrangements without worrying, "Is this going to make someone cry?"

GRUBER: How have the solos and music and the relationships onstage evolved day to day?

HAMILTON: For me, Monday was the most exciting night because it was all brand new and happening for the first time. Day Two you fall into the trap of, 'oh, we've already done this,' almost harder work. Day Three, we've done this twice so we felt a bit more solid and it's getting better and better.

GRUBER: My experience with day two, you all seemed more relaxed and having more fun.

HAMILTON: Yeah, you've already gone through the experience of meeting all of the challenges of the music, so you know you are up to the test and it's just a question of concentration. Once a certain competence level is reached, it's all about staying focused and in the moment and not missing information, what's happening. And that's not just about reading the music in front of you, it's about listening to the music round about you, reacting appropriately.

GRUBER: How do you prepare, both when you first get the music and before each show?

HAMILTON: I got the music while I was traveling. If I am at home, I can take the music and have a look at it. This time it was different, so I packed a keyboard in my suitcase just big enough, three octaves, to load the music up on the iPad and then just play. Guy sent out little demonstration files of all the charts, this is what it could look like. I knew most of the tunes but *Le Lis* and *Funky Thide of Sings*, we hadn't done that.

GRUBER: Well he said onstage he hadn't done *Funky Thide* live for, what, 40 years?

HAMILTON: Well, let's see, I'm 43, so yeah, I wouldn't have done that (*laughter*). And then there were things subtly altered by Guy's arrangements. Most of the time he is expanding for soloists or he will pick up on a theme; he has a couple of musically eloquent introductions like *Red Baron* which just sets the whole thing up. You get the enjoyment of being a part of it, of influencing the direction. But you don't get the listener enjoyment of it. I have a nice sound in my headphones but when you are on stage you never get to experience the full effect of what it's meant to sound like. It's something people forget when they talk about recording and what things should sound like from a musician's point of view. Musicians usually get the worst experience of the sound in the whole room. If you're sitting behind the drum set, you're never going to hear that balance to the same degree as somebody who is sitting out front. Your own instrument is right there. Even the physicality of an acoustic piano, if somebody is sitting playing a solo piano concert, they are behind the keyboard but the piano is designed to throw sound off the lid out into the audience. So, all the frequencies, the quality of the sound, you never get to hear a piano properly and yet you play your entire life.

GRUBER: One of the trombone players joked that he lost two percent of his hearing sitting in front of the trumpeters the first night of the show.

HAMILTON: That's why I consider myself a listener of music first and then a player, because I am always trying to hear from the audience's perspective.

GRUBER: When you listen to *Spectrum*, or to Mahavishnu, what was unique about Bill's work with Jan Hammer as a music fan and a keyboardist? What made Jan special?

HAMILTON: Everything about Jan was special. He had an uncanny understanding of complex odd-time signatures which these days is not as rare as it was back then. There were only a handful of people in that world who could speak that language. So, when people heard that language spoken, it was almost like...if you look at the other great keyboard players from that era, Chick Corea, Herbie Hancock, none of them played in an odd-time signature. I hate to say it but it's true. It's not a criticism. There are not any Chick Corea tunes where he is soloing in seven, same with Herbie, but somebody like Jan, because he grew up in that culture, that's second nature. So, you have, "Hey Jan, meet Billy," Billy can also play in that language and they created this whole genre, you know. And then his control of all the different sounds. It's fearlessness. It's deciding this is the voice I want to use. And these guys getting their hands on all of this technology when it was all brand new, literally just being invented by some really innovative people. It's an amazing moment in music history. I'm pretty sure they still had to tune all the oscillators before each take and sometimes they'll drift a little bit. That just makes it sound even better to me.

GRUBER: What are the respective styles of Guy and Bill as band leaders? What's been your experience with Guy?

HAMILTON: Guy was in one of the first bands I toured with when I was about 17-years-old. So, I got to play with him back then for weeks and weeks and hang out with him. He was fantastic, one of the most upbeat, music-loving, forward-thinking individuals, but he didn't arrange, he was a trumpet player, then a band leader in his own right. He did a record deal with Verve, getting a lot of attention, but is now known as an arranger. Says he doesn't play much these days but has always been a great trumpet player.

GRUBER: He seems to be having a lot of fun playing.

HAMILTON: He is having a great time. There are very few people in the world who could have done what he did with these arrangements because there is a balancing act. What a lot of arrangers want to do is make everything theirs, put their signature on it and alter so many things so you lose the original intention. Guy has been very careful and respectful of Billy's ideas whilst molding it gently into his own designs.

GRUBER: When you see Guy's sheet music for *Stratus*, for example, what is recognizable and what is not?

HAMILTON: He spoke to me in advance. What he has done was to take what Jan Hammer played and expanded that for big band. Not what Jan played as a solo but as an accompanist. All these rhythmic things happening and chords happening that are transcribed from what Jan played and then spread throughout the band. It's like *Stratus* stretched out on a big elastic band.

GRUBER: What was your reaction to the opening to *Red Baron*?

HAMILTON: That's like a little opus unto itself. Almost like James Bond-esque moments. Very classy.

GRUBER: How do you communicate onstage? What are some subtle forms of communication you have with Bill, Guy and other band members?

HAMILTON: I try to stay open all the time. I try not to go on autopilot. Playing with Bill is like getting a free master class every night. He will do something different every night that he didn't do before.

GRUBER: What is the importance of having fun onstage?

HAMILTON: It's like boxing. You do all the preparation before the main event, that's where the hard work is done. By the time you get to the stage...Bill said something good about that. If you pay money to see a band, do you want to see a bunch of uptight guys who are really serious and not having fun, and how is that going to sound, or do you want to see a bunch of guys who are relaxed and happy and make it look effortless? Music isn't just about making sound, it's a sharing of energy with other people.

I ask Steve how he started in music.

HAMILTON: ... started music young, Dad was a musician, he taught me. I took lessons with piano teachers, then won a scholarship to study at Berklee College of Music where I met amazing musicians like Antonio Sanchez who worked with Pat Metheny and did the *Birdman* soundtrack. Phil Collins paid for my tuition which seemed to set my destiny.

There's a knock at the door. A waiter enters and picks up plates holding the remains of the pre-show dinner.

GRUBER: How did the Phil Collins relationship come about?

HAMILTON: We had no money as a family. So, my mum had written lots of letters to people asking for sponsorship. I got an amazing letter back from Dudley Moore, he wasn't in a position to help, but was very complimentary about the music and I told him I was a fan of Derek and Clive. I don't know if you…

GRUBER: I have. It's the most vulgar shit I have ever heard in my life (*laughter*).

HAMILTON: He wrote I am glad that Derek and Clive had some socially redeeming qualities. I ended up not long after moving to London, joining Bill Bruford's band. Bruford was an old colleague of Phil's and his wife was still in touch with Phil's family and they were exchanging messages about me and they said, hey guess what, this Scottish kid just joined Bill's band.

GRUBER: How was it working with Bill Bruford?

HAMILTON: I did that band for five or six years and we did a massive amount of traveling; we toured the States five or six times.

GRUBER: When was that?

HAMILTON: All through the late '90s to 2003, 2004. We did four CDs, a live double-album, a live DVD from the Bottom Line in New York. I co-wrote a lot of the music with Bill.

GRUBER: Were you a Yes or King Crimson fan?

HAMILTON: No, and it turns out that's one of the reasons I got the gig, because I didn't know anything, so I wasn't going to annoy him with questions. Bill said, we're here to do this thing but once it's done I just want some peace and quiet and don't want to be answering 100 questions about Robert Fripp. It was only years later that I realized there was a heavy progressive rock legacy.

Bill Bruford and Tricksy Meters

In reaching out to musicians for their remembrances and thoughts on Bill's impact on world music, many had arcane layers of management and contact systems. Bill Bruford, legendary progressive rock drummer with Yes and King Crimson, then jazz composer and bandleader, then author and Ph.D. candidate, responded quickly and kindly with this anecdote.

BILL BRUFORD: I sure remember my first encounter with Billy. It was at Pritchard Gymnasium, SUNY Stony Brook, November 28th, 1971. I was in Yes, and we were in rapid ascent around that time, touring hard. We were due to support the Kinks that night, and some weird Orchestra (led by Murray Vishnu as Tony Levin's mother had it) had been a last-minute addition to open the show. I was only dimly aware of both Billy and the Mahavishnu Orchestra, although I loved John McLaughlin's work from back home in the UK, especially on *Extrapolation*.

We turn up to the gig and look for the dressing room. There's a big drum kit, maybe even two kick drums, nicely set up by the side of the stage, waiting for action. As I walk past I tap each drum once with my finger tips to check the sound, as you do; very sweet, beautifully tuned. Murray Vishnu obviously wasn't going to be Black Sabbath. This was going to be interesting.

Before they go on stage, the band members gather around a drum in the dressing room where they count and clap rhythms in some highly tricksy meters I'd never met before. I listen outside for a bit, and when they hit the stage, all heaven breaks loose. I gather our keyboard player Rick Wakeman and march him out to the house, saying, "You'd better come and hear this."

The band is sensational; on top of their game, playing with a conviction that I was later to recognise within King Crimson, the conviction that you're on to something, and you can't put a foot wrong. Wakeman doesn't see it. I had to stop listening after a while; it was too good.

I didn't dare say hello to Billy that night, or invade their dressing room - way too much respect for that - but of course I followed Billy and the band from afar. *Spectrum* gave me the strength to do *Feels Good to Me*.

He Is Always Showing Me Stuff

I meet Santiago Roberts on the stage to get a better understanding of the drum set-up and the nature of his relationship with Bill.

ROBERTS: 360 Evans, now we are switching to G2's, these two are EC2's, still double ply. Two bass drums, Evans E60. Once he chooses the scale he wants to be in, he will tune the bass drum a fifth interval below from the root key.

GRUBER: The first time I saw you in Acton, you were sitting on the floor with the anvil. What's your role? Student, intern, roadie?

ROBERTS: All of those. When I first 'met' Billy, my mom gave me the *Spectrum* album when I was 10.

GRUBER: She had good taste.

ROBERTS: She didn't know what the hell it was. She went to the store and asked which were the two best drummers right now. A very trippy Dennis Chambers *Uncle Moe's Space Ranch*. And *Spectrum*. I started banging around when I was six or seven. When I was eight, my father gave me a small electronic Yamaha. I was the youngest of six, so had to steal my brother's albums.

I always knew about Bill. After the show at The Mint, I just went over to take a picture. For some strange reason, he said 'wait till I sign stuff.' I was studying at LA College of Music, beginning of my last quarter. Was waiting for 17 years to see this guy. My dad loves jazz. He had never been to a jazz fusion concert. Loved it. He also wanted to talk to Billy. Me being a smartass, I said I could set up a clinic back in Costa Rica, which I had never done. Gave me his email and I wrote to him, never thinking he would write back. A few days later, he writes back.

GRUBER: Why did you think he wrote back?

ROBERTS: I thought we needed more people like Billy to come over there to show us how to do stuff. That is reflected when you have integrity on your intentions. I was relaxed and being in school, in my last quarter. Costa Ricans have a tendency to sell their country a lot, we are all tourist guides in a way

GRUBER: *Pura vida.* When I was here on Monday you were very busy setting things up. How does Bill's set up differ from other drummers?

ROBERTS: He has used three kinds of heads just this week. He is always experimenting.

I ask Santiago why he thinks Bill does a lot of the physical work himself. Is that because he is humble, because he likes to be physically involved in the pursuit of perfection?

ROBERTS: All of those and with him, he is always showing me stuff. He will send me exercises, 'this is in three, try to think about it in 11.' In school, you learn techniques. Bill's exercises are active, working muscles and using the whole body. First exercise was to put two Bibles under my arms and put a quarter on the practice pad and practice the rudiments just by using my forearms. You activate more muscles so the bridge between what you think and execute is shorter. That really helped me with precision. And that's why it's so important to have good posture. Don't be a rhythmatist, be a musician.

GRUBER: What about the problem they were having during load-in?

ROBERTS: The legs for the floor toms were missing. We had to set everything up first and called the area store. These are not the ones for the specific model but they still work.

GRUBER: I have seen people freak out for much less.

ROBERTS: He was completely chill. Even with a 17-piece band. He has a good sense of humor. He makes everyone feel comfortable with a funny comment.

Mesmerized

Guitarist Carl Orr settles in for dinner backstage. I ask him how the show is going.

CARL ORR: Very good. Skills required are a lot different. In a small group, I take a lot more solos. There is a lot of reading involved. I'm a competent reader but not super-fast like some of these guys. I spend most of my time with my eyes on the page. A little bit outside of my comfort zone. I'm known as an improviser and writer, a composer and an ensemble player. Different from somebody like McLaughlin or Pat Metheny, I really am part of the rhythm section.

My dad told me to read biographies of great musicians to find out how they tick. I (read) about mentoring in the world of jazz, Miles Davis going to New York, onstage training with Charlie Parker, then Miles being a mentor. I found a great musician in Sydney, Jackie Orszacky, a Hungarian-born bass player and composer. Closest thing we had to Miles in Australia. I actively sought training as a rhythm guitarist. I was an improviser already. Any guitarist wants to play solos. Jackie said to me one day, don't play on the same part of the bar as the bass and drums. Put the guitar in between there. Guitar becomes the glue that cements the rhythm section. I really love being that guy.

GRUBER: On stage last night, I noticed Bill and Michael making eye contact and laughing. How are you communicating onstage as a rhythm section?

ORR: Not much eye contact. I look around at Bill (Carl's chair is stage right, directly in front of Bill). He has his head full of a lot of things and I am just one of the components, especially in this large group, so I just lock myself in to Bill's drum kit.

I ask what Carl means by that.

ORR: I listen intently to what Bill is playing all the time. I listen to everything that's going on around me and I put my guitar playing into that rather than listening to myself first.

GRUBER: Jan Hammer said that he and McLaughlin had the freedom to go off in the directions that they did and innovate and experiment because Bill provided the driving structure and foundation.

ORR: Sure. Yeah, he still does. One of the things I like about Bill is he makes things really clear. One of the idiotic games that musicians play is what you might call 'hide the beat.' Trying to be so polyrhythmic and tricky that the audience loses their place; musicians also might lose their place. Bill never does that. Bill will play the most advanced things but he will always, always make things clear.

GRUBER: When is the first time you heard Bill's music?

ORR: On one track on a Milt Jackson album. Phenomenal CTI record. The track featured Bill, Freddie Hubbard, Herbie Hancock and Ron Carter.

GRUBER: Quite a lineup.

ORR: It was the first jazz record I ever bought, when I was 14-years-old. Then I bought his (Milt Jackson's) previous album called *Sunflower*, which they were playing here last night.

Milt Jackson, legendary vibraphonist, released *Sunflower* in early 1973, the year of *Spectrum's* release and the third and final year of the original Mahavishnu Orchestra.

GRUBER: That was in Sydney?

ORR: In Adelaide. I thought, the way I am going to learn about jazz is listening to the radio, and the first thing that attracts my attention, I am going to write the title down and I am going to go out and buy it. And I did. And that was the first one. My familiarity with Bill began with the first jazz record I ever bought.

On my 15th birthday, I spent my money on *Inner Mounting Flame* by Mahavishnu and I thought, is this the guy on that Milt Jackson record?!?! I was really taken aback. I was amazed and I loved it. Bill had a kind of funkiness that I liked. You know, Mahavishnu Orchestra was very strange music. Amazing but strange. But Bill had an earthy funkiness, more like the pop and funk music that I was familiar with.

GRUBER: What was your first impression of *Spectrum*?

ORR: I remember clearly the first time I heard it. I was about 17 and had a jam with some musicians a few years older. One of the guys said, "Aw, hey, you gotta hear this album, man." I remember being mesmerized by it.

GRUBER: As a guitarist, was there something unique about the interplay between Tommy Bolin, Jan and Bill for you?

ORR: Tommy was a straight-up rock guitarist. It was great for me to hear a very adventurous and advanced form of jazz played with instruments familiar to me. Sonically, it wasn't a million miles away from Led Zeppelin and Pink Floyd, closer to that sound than Charlie Parker or Kenny Burrell for that matter.

> *He can write amazing melodies. I like the way he puts guitar in the center. He knows how to play straightaway jazz but he is a rocker too. This is one of the guys who created jazz-rock. When I started to listen to fusion bands like Weather Report, it could be difficult to understand what they were playing if you were not familiar with that genre. When I heard Spectrum, I was directly seduced. Even if the music is complicated, it's easy to listen to, and accessible to a big audience. I'm not surprised it was one of the biggest successes in jazz-rock history. That album is a good combination of sophisticated and punchy, straight music. Since that period, Billy's music has combined sophistication, great grooves, and great melodies.*
>
> *— Jean-Marie Ecay, French jazz guitarist, frequent Cobham band member*

GRUBER: You hang around jazz musicians. Do you think for some of them this was heretical, that these guys were somehow degrading the...

ORR: Well, look what happened. This kind of puritanical conservative approach really dismissed the value of that music. Just like Margaret Thatcher, same time and same behavior. Just telling people, you're wrong, here is the way things are supposed to be done, really horrific. Herbie Hancock pointed out the similarities between politics and the musical landscape. I don't think it's a coincidence that these things happen at the same time.

GRUBER: 1970s…

ORR: Well, look at it, yeah…

GRUBER: There was a ferment around social issues, race, the Vietnam War, gender issues, at the same time as there was this fusion with jazz and rock.

ORR: Definitely.

GRUBER: There was a disruption, a transformation in the social and political landscape.

ORR: Jazz historically, sorry, I want to use an extreme…

GRUBER: Bring it on, Carl.

ORR: Men in dull gray suits, what are you doing that's so compelling that I am supposed to latch on? I've been reading a new book, *Duke Ellington's America*, Duke was the biggest selling black artist in the 1930's.

GRUBER: That's when jazz was pop.

ORR: Yeah, and later on there was Louis Armstrong, Count Basie. Modern jazz came along and then fusion was kind of bringing it back to all that, "Why don't we pay attention to what's happening in popular music?" Herbie did it with funk as well. I thought it was a great thing. Playing jazz on electric guitars with big amps and distortion brought it into a familiar soundscape that regular people were used to. Also, it allowed for forms of musical exploration and development that weren't possible before.

GRUBER: How do you prepare for a show like this?

ORR: First, I am a practicing Buddhist. (*We greet bassist Michael Mondesir as he walks into the backstage lounge and invite him to the conversation.*) So, I practice chanting for at least an hour a day. Two to three if possible. I go through this music, the tricky bits. One of the best pieces of advice I ever had was, don't keep practicing the stuff you can play, make a note of the bits you are having difficulty with and practice them. I remember reading Dizzy Gillespie's autobiography, *To Be or Not to Bop*, and he said whenever people ask me how much do you practice, I reply, every spare minute. I've got to do things as a dad…

MONDESIR: You've got a life! You are allowed!

ORR: Yeah, I've got a life. I try to get to the gig early so I am in the best possible state of mind.

GRUBER: I asked Bill how he prepared before a Yoshi's gig a while back and he said, I watch cartoons.

ORR: Yeah, but that's the only 20 minutes he gets to relax all day. Bill prepares by being Bill.

GRUBER: How does your Buddhism serve your preparation or for being a guitarist on stage? Strength, breathing, relaxation, focus?

ORR: It helps me to focus my mind and to relax but also the Buddhist philosophy is helpful, respecting everybody equally, the equal dignity of all people.

GRUBER: Do you meditate?

ORR: Chanting. Nichiren Buddhism. I was reading about Art Blakey, he was not a Buddhist, but his attitude was in line with Buddhism. He said, gentlemen, we have a mission - that's very much a Buddhist attitude - and the mission is, make the world a better place, a nicer, happier place to live in for everyone. Art Blakey was really clear; we have a mission to bring this music to people. It's about me doing my best for everybody.

GRUBER: Michael, how do you prepare for a show?

MONDESIR: I prepare for all kinds of playing in context. This week is brand new charts. I can read music - only eight years now - I am not as strong a reader as the horn guys. That's what they do from 12-years-old onwards, always hitting it. I had 23 years of totally using ears and memory;

luckily, I have very good memory and OK ears. Generally, if I have learned something, then I really know it.

Carl asks if anyone wants to order from the musician's short list menu. Mike tells Carl he wants the same as last night. He interjects, "Nobody else I know has the ability to do that."

MONDESIR: (Brother) Mark has a strong ear. We both have an innate thing in terms of playing rhythm. It isn't something we practiced or studied. Upon hearing Bill and Mahavishnu, to us it was immediately obvious that it was home. Somebody understands us! After years of people saying, what's wrong with you guys, I need to be in another room. Hearing Jan Hammer improvise and how he places things rhythmically, that was closest to how I naturally hear.

(Carl leaves the room.)

I was in The Strand doing *Dream Girls*. Trying to learn a musical, it really is another thing, playing-wise. They are not hard lines, not millions of notes; some of Bill's new stuff has torrents of notes. *(Mike scats a long stream of notes)* They have bar changes to tie in with the words. Some strange things, a bar of one. It is really important to learn every note. The talking and everything that is happening. Then just roughly use the charts.

GRUBER: I noticed last night in the second set, you and Bill were laughing and smiling at each other, maybe just enjoying the music. How important is communication for the rhythm section? What happens on stage between you, Bill, Steve, and Carl?

MONDESIR: It's everything. I am very lucky that how I came to playing was that I heard Bill and it turned on this thing that said, I am a musician. I play the bass. Quite literally that. Everything that I have played before meeting him comes from how he phrases, so playing is extremely comfortable. With Bill, it is really honed so it is not a struggle to find where he is. There are things that I am not as strong at. I think that I could be stronger in the slower tempos, the long notes, I am completely aware of it and strive to improve. Communication-wise there is quite a lot of laughing happening because we are both aware, there is a lot of humor in it. Bill could play a phrase that really only he and I do, 'that's from this,' or I could physically trip up, screw up the line then come back, because I don't see, I am definitely not the most technically gifted player. I'm the bassist in the band. There are times I could trip up and quite often it is my mechanical deficiencies rather than not having a clue where I am. I could play and it comes out wrong, but I am aware, then stop, *bang*, and I am straight in the right place. If that happens, Bill is aware and he will laugh. That is an example when there is comedy.

GRUBER: In Brazil, you told me a story while we were riding in a van to the gig about Bill's influence on you as a young man and how you came to play with him.

MONDESIR: Mark played drums pretty regularly, started at 12. I was playing as well at 11, always really loved drums, but I didn't really have the drive to practice. Both Mark and I, as well as our big sister Val, were prodigious artists. Everyone thought Mark would play the drums and I would draw. When Mark reached 16 - I am a year younger - this friend of a friend told us about Bill, you have to hear this guy, he has *'arms like tree trunks'* and he is really fast and crazy. Mark got a couple of albums from the local record library and played them. To both of us, it was like, "This is the thing, this is us." Everything back then was on the radio. Today it's all playlists and very narrow, but back then you heard everything, Laura Nyro, Roy Wood, King Crimson, Beatles, Stones, plus at home we had the classic Caribbean household thing of calypso, and country and western. They are both storytelling styles. You heard a lot of Charley Pride, Jim Reeves…

I express my astonishment that Caribbean households in London loved American country music.

MONDESIR: Big time. Wholesale and retail. It's all connected, happens in rock and roll as well, but with our parents, country was number one and calypso, so we naturally came from that. Really listening widely from the radio. The *Shabazz* live album was 1974, that was the first we heard, that lineup was crazy, it instantly hit us. Not long after, someone told us he was playing at Hammersmith Odeon in London. We had to go. Mark was trying to play how Bill played off the records, not having clarity on how he had his hands, hearing constant rolls with hi-hat as well. He is trying to play the things he is hearing but didn't know what was happening. So, catching him live and looking at him hi-hat with left hand, snare with the right, it really clicked, "Ah, that's obvious now."

Guy Barker walks in to greetings all round.

That evening, we hung around backstage and he came out. At this point, I had not touched a bass, but I knew I could play one. I don't know how I knew but I knew. I told him, "In 10 years, I will be playing with you." Some tiny kid with a huge afro who could hardly talk (Michael and brother Mark sometimes stutter). His response was, "Yeah, OK, it's a deal." (*Laughter*) So, I'm going, "Great." Unfortunately, that did not happen in 10 years. It happened in 11 years. The concert must have been 1982 and I got to play on the *Traveler* album, mid-end of 1993.

GRUBER: How did you connect with him?

MONDESIR: He called me. At my mum's house. On the landline. A school friend of ours, Derek Pattie, the most hilarious human on the planet, a wise-cracking, wind-up kind of guy, was always ringing up, doing voices, "This is Miles," etcetera. Bill rings my mum's house, and I answer it, and, "This is Bill Cobham," and I say, "Fuck off Derek." And Bill goes, "Who's Derek??" I could hardly speak. "So-so-so-so sorry, I have this friend . . ." and he says, "That's OK. I am in England at the moment recording at Real World and are you interesting in recording?" "Oh (*laughter*), I'll just look at my diary and I'll just have my people... Yeah, yes, yes."

Mike tells Bill that charts are not really going to help because he could not read music, so Bill sends audio. "I came in, played on three tracks, he's happy after that and I thought, oh, he's happy!" In 1995, Bill calls again asking if Mike is around to play some concerts at the Jazz Cafe. Mike plays on what he calls "rescue missions," about twice a year till 2003. Then, early 2009, Mike plays for Bill again, and is asked if he wants to be a member of the band.

Food is arriving, and I insist that Mike eat as we talk. I ask why *Stratus* is considered one of the classic bass lines. For Bill's 70th birthday video, I recorded some friends and musicians offering well-wishes from around the world. Renowned bassist Marcus Miller played the opening to *Stratus* as he wished Bill a happy birthday. Mike says Marcus' birthday was the day before and Carl mentions that he jammed with Marcus on *Stratus*. "I was there for that!" declares Mike.

MONDESIR: There's not really another line like it. It's a continuous line. And it's almost all one note. But, two other notes are in there, *do do do da do de da*. Really, even now, not another line as driving as that. Bill's placement is really like no one else's, so you are creating this tunnel. This is heading *here* and *nobody's gonna stop it*. You can't help but have your head moving. It's earthy, incredibly grounded. There are other lines like it but there is some kind of rest. This is literally the whole time.

GRUBER: You don't have arms like tree trunks (*laughter*) so...

MONDESIR: (*Laughs and extends his arms*) I don't even have arms! You're saying I'm not a macho man?? Is that what you're driving at, Brian?

GRUBER: Does it require a technique to be driving those same notes through the entire piece? Even listening to it, my left hand gets tired.

MONDESIR: I like the line. How I play, I pluck the notes and hold them. I play quite lightly, I try to play high intensity, low energy.

ORR: Low exertion.

MONDESIR: Quite a lot of players, this is how they pluck (*demonstrates an aggressive style*). And I'm like this (*plucks lightly*). I learned to execute like that by having a look at Bill, because he plays with a lot of power and a lot of energy, but he isn't over-exerting. He is floating around so I thought that is how you are supposed to execute.

Guy is organizing his materials and I ask if I am in his way on the couch.

BARKER: I'm good actually. I did a lot of work today. I did a bit of practice and I did quite a bit more on my cello project. Yeah, tomorrow I'm going to be a good boy and go to yoga and write the rest of the day.

Silverware and plates clink noisily as people dig in.

GRUBER: How was last night's show for you?

BARKER: I loved it. I'm just going to do a bit of editing, the sax part of *Sal Si Puedes*. So that they can stay alive.

MONDESIR: It's a bit of a mad line. I can play it because I am not having to inhale. (*Carl asks Mike if he'd like something to drink.*) If there is sparkling water. I am so highbrow.

ORR: This water is gently sparkling.

MONDESIR: It's not delightful though.

The conversation turns to physical preparation and exercise.

BARKER: I do Bikram yoga. After three months of it, I got my trumpet out one morning, same routine, same warmup, and, something...*what happened just there?* I used to have to take a breath in the middle. Now I've just gone all the way through without thinking about it. When I was 19 or 20, I went to New York, went to all the teachers, obsessed with getting better. I went to Charles Colin. He said, "What do you want?" I said, "The only way I can get better is I need to practice more hours in the day. To get my stamina up." He said, "Go swimming." I thought, "I don't want to hear that. I want the magic solution." He said, "Your body plays the note. Ninety-five percent of the muscles in your body all come into action, down to your calves."

A hundred years later, when I was doing that exercise, I realized how right he was. In the end, going to yoga was like doing another hour's trumpet practice. The best thing he ever said to me, and I will always remember it, was when he said, "OK, play a C scale." So I played a fairly ordinary C scale. He said, "No. Guy, you are on the stage of Carnegie Hall, I am on the front row of the balcony. On the program, it says 'C scale.' And that's what you have to play. So, stand up there, close your eyes, see me in the balcony and play me a C scale." And out poured a very grand C scale. (*Sings the C scale*). "There you go," he said. "The trumpet hates inconsistency. So, never practice. Always perform."

A Flirtation with Lyrics

GRUBER: I was listening to *Drum 'n' Voice Volume Four* while driving to Phoenix a few weeks ago. I loved it and was surprised to hear lyrics to your music. Have you thought about doing more with the spoken word?

COBHAM: No, because I didn't feel comfortable. You need to ask the guy who wrote them, Gregg Kofi Brown, lead singer of an African band (Osibisa). I wrote something called *Puffnstuff*, haven't played it since 1980, about the whole scene with drugs. I was playing with Alvin Baptiste in New Orleans who turned me on to Randy Jackson, who played bass, then went on to play with Whitney Houston and Journey. He was on the *American Idol* panel, came out of Southern University in Baton Rouge. Charlie Singleton, lead guitar, who left for a funk band called Cameo. Ray Mouton, from eastern Louisiana. Sounded a lot like George Benson in those days. Mark Soskin was the keyboard player, teaches now at the Manhattan School of Music. It was an amazing time, thought it was a great way to work. I had a guy in the band, Kenneth Kamal Scott, a singer, incredible falsetto voice. Wrote a tune on one of my albums, *Simplicity of Expression, Depth of Thought* called *Early Libra*. Never played it again, never felt comfortable with the lyric thing. I wrote the lyrics for a Mark Soskin tune called *Bolinas*. I was living in Mill Valley (San Francisco Bay Area) 1975- '79. That place made me feel amazing. Then we had an earthquake and my retaining wall cracked. I said, OK, this is a sign I should leave.

I call Gregg Kofi Brown, now living in London, to find out more about the lyrics collaboration. As with many others, he has a unique story about Bill's effect on his musical life.

BROWN: On the last *Drum 'n' Voice*, there are three songs that I co-wrote, performing on at least two. I first met Billy in the mid '80's. I had an '86-'87 hit in America at the time, *Baby Talk*. A 17-year-old Italian girl in NY, Elisha, recorded it. I was a bass player, worked with Eric Burdon, Joe Cocker. At that time, we all listened to Billy Cobham, Weather Report, Return to Forever.

GRUBER: Let me ask you what I asked Michael Mondesir. Why is *Stratus* considered a classic bassline?

BROWN: A rolling bass line tests your chops. When I taught bass at Southhampton Solent University, I told students to play something consistent for five to 10 minutes, test your mettle. With *Stratus,* you got to hold that groove, one amazing song in terms of holding that pocket. I had a house with my band in LA, like an army camp for these issues. Bill was our hero; to all these guys, he was like God.

GRUBER: What struck you about playing with him?

BROWN: He is up there with Miles, his impact on people's playing (*mentions Massive Attack's sample of Stratus on Safe from Harm*), he has worked with the greatest musicians on the planet. That is his legacy. From working with the Fania All-Stars, to Mahavishnu.

GRUBER: Any moments where you were inspired by the music to write certain lyrics, alone or together? Tell me about your process with Bill.

BROWN: I have got a kind of solitary process, my best work I do on my own. I'm like a writer, like you, writing a book. I like to meditate and listen to the music and get into the vibe of it. Me knowing Bill and having played with him, that is enough to inspire me, getting my work done. I have always done my best work, writing songs for Dennis Chambers, Stanley Jordan, me on my own.

Bill sent me a song one time, he wanted me to write some lyrics for him. I thought he said, write around a title, *Defecated Coconut*. So, I am writing this song about defecated coconut (*laughter*). Needless to say, it didn't get used. I was like, *what the hell is that about?* Bill said, *"No, Greg,* it was *desiccated* coconuts, man!!"

The previous songs for *Drum 'n' Voice 1 & 2*, I co-wrote, not specifically written for Bill. The *Drum 'n' Voice Volume Four* songs were written specifically for Bill.

Shadow was one of the more successful songs for Bill commercially, CBS loved that song, put it on a compilation album *More Smooth Jazz on a Summer's Day* with Luther Vandross, Stanley Clarke. Tom Scott, Richard

Bona, Grover Washington, Ramsey Lewis, Gato Barbieri, Tower of Power. That album did quite well. I wrote that song with the producers before knowing it would go on Bill's song on the album.

Superstar was written with Bill in mind, lovely track, certainly *Joy, Le Lis*. Bill is part of a tradition back to the early 1900s with Jelly Roll Morton, all the way up to the present. To me, Bill represents that legacy of jazz, which was popular music in the '30s, '40s, that legacy of pop music, black music in particular, that harks back to the slave calls, all the way up through blues, jazz, Latin jazz. *Superstar* represents the continuum of that legacy of African music, a continuum up until today. That song has got a young R&B singer and a young rapper from London. In terms of youth culture, London is one of the most important places on the planet. All these people have come to London like Jay-Z to see what is happening with the youth in London to bring things back to America. Drum and bass, dubstep, all these new musical genres, youth-culture wise, even if you go back to the *Beatles* and *Stones*, they took African-American music and turned it around and sold it back to the Anglo-American community. Anglos had this music in their backyard all the time but a lot of them were not exposed to it because of racial and social divides. It took these British-Anglo bands and artists to educate America about African-American music. I learned more about African-American music reading stories about Eric Clapton than I did in schools. And I lived in Memphis and California and Alaska. So, I had quite a variety of experiences growing up, but certainly, that song *Superstar* represents a continuum of music into now.

6 AND ON THE SIXTH DAY

I meet Bill Saturday afternoon for our final interview over lunch at the Scoff and Banter Bloomsbury, to see what stories may have as yet gone untold and to ask how he feels the week has gone.

COBHAM: Much better than I expected but I don't know what I expected. One of the best bands I have ever played in.

GRUBER: Best big band?

COBHAM: Overall, the best big band I ever played with. They solo well and they really gel together. Guy put together these guys based on how he wrote. In comparison, he wrote for the hr Bigband, but those were the guys who were there, that's all he had to work with. Whereas, say, for example, the trumpet section; he knew that he would need three first chair players and not 1, 2, 3, and 4 players to play the parts. Why, because he needed them to spell each other in the upper register because of the way the music was written. He knew exactly who to call to do that. You can't buy that.

GRUBER: Tell me about the players.

COBHAM: We got the guys. Guy acquired the right people to make the right impression. As long as we got all of the notes right, it's cool. He also knew things that I could never begin to bring to the table. A lot of my music is not written for wind players. So, he had to split up the parts to spell, and give these guys a chance to breathe and sustain their stamina, pace themselves throughout the show.

GRUBER: There were some great dueling solos. There's a passage in Geoff Dyer's classic jazz book *But Beautiful* about Coleman Hawkins and Lester Young cutting each other for eight hours.

I poke around my Kindle app until I find the passage, then share it with Bill.

> *When they jammed together Hawk tried everything he knew to cut him but he never managed it. In Kansas in '34 they played right through the morning, Hawk stripped down to his singlet, trying to blow him down with that big hurricane tenor, and Lester slumped in a chair with that faraway look in his eyes, his tone still light as a breeze after eight hours' playing. The pair of them wore out pianists until there was no one left and Hawk walked off the stand, threw his horn in the back of his car, and gunned it all the way to St. Louis for that night's gig.* [18]

GRUBER: So, when you have Guy and Nigel playing off each other…

COBHAM: That's called trading. They were trading eights, trading fours. (*Starts clapping and scatting to emulate two horns trading riffs*). They're having a conversation. Those guys were off the hook man. They can play.

GRUBER: Mike Hobart of the *Financial Times* said he has never seen three trombonists in one band solo like that.

COBHAM: (*Laughs*) Serious, serious shit. You don't realize how much…What happens is these guys get forced to play up to the standards of the others. If there is a weak link in the process, they are getting better and better and better. If he doesn't have that kind of platform, he ends up going down the rabbit hole and getting weaker and weaker.

GRUBER: After the shows when you were signing CDs, was there any memorable feedback?

COBHAM: The general feedback was in the same category, never seen anything like it. What a band. That's where you want to be, what I teach fundamentally, that you are part of a group.

---

[18] Dyer, Geoff. *2014. But Beautiful: A Book About Jazz.* North Point Press. Kindle edition, location 141.

GRUBER: It's an ambitious program, having Guy arrange complex music for 17 people.

COBHAM: I had no clear hopes. Just to be successful in the presentation. It's gone way beyond that. I think it's always about trusting your gut. That feeling you have that this could work. That's always been my large credo. "Looks like it could happen. I'll take a shot at it."

GRUBER: Well, the audience loved it. The Ronnie Scott's guys loved it. The *Financial Times* guy loved it.

COBHAM: One of the things I found in my life with music, that keeps me coming back more and more, now past the obsession part, when you do the things you believe in, it will come out as a positive no matter what it is you do. It is a language that will not lie. I suspect that's why in some areas of the world they don't want music involved in their social environment because it tells the truth.

GRUBER: When you hear music that inspires you, how do you experience it emotionally, physically, intellectually?

COBHAM: I tend to retain it for a very long time, in my mind's eye, obsessed. When people are driving with me, it's like being in a morgue. The music is in my head, a lot of different things are playing in sequence, I can drive quiet for hours. People ask, "Are you all right?" My brain is like on overdrive. I look at the score the first day, after that I will be playing from memory. I wish I could do that as effectively in other areas of my life.

GRUBER: Was any of your touring government-supported?

COBHAM: No.

GRUBER: You did UNICEF.

COBHAM: I did once come to a project through the Italian government. It was just, wow, this guy works well with people who have mental health issues, what would happen if you put him together with them in a good way. The seed was sown there in Trieste. I was there with a doctor, loved what I was doing as a fan. She asked, can you come to Trieste with Nigerian Yoruba percussionists. We went down to test with 200 outpatients from a local sanitarium and put on a show. Marble floor, beautiful Italian building, archway, high ceilings, beautiful sound and we just played drums. They were not really that interested. The dancers went away and we kept playing, and, all of a sudden, lot of people got out of their seats and put their bodies on the floor just to feel the vibration. A lot of those people who did that had not spoken for over 50 years to anyone outside of the people where they were kept. They were silent because they had no rhythmic or tonal key that allowed them to feel comfortable about speaking about how they were or what they saw. They were 75-80 years old, speaking old Italian, words not used for 20-30 years.

GRUBER: When was that?

COBHAM: 1992. It started with that. Next thing you know we were down in Rome. I made a last record for Creed Taylor at CTI around that date. He produced Stan Getz, all the bossa nova stuff was Creed. Out of the blue, I get a call from my then-manager Nancy Meyers, says Creed needs you to do a project for Pioneer Laserdisc in Japan.

Before I could go there, I had a mandate to go to Salvador de Bahia (Brazil) to rehearse with a band and then go down to Santos to work with street people for UNICEF out of Florence, based on this project. The project got accepted by UNICEF but the Nigerians could not come because of visa problems and went back to the city of Bayreuth (Bavaria, Germany). We were working there in the Wagner opera house in non-western music, run by a foundation for non-western art. Unbelievable, really rich period.

GRUBER: When you were onstage this week telling the story behind *Eggshells*, were you referring back to that time?

COBHAM: Yes, yes. Those were the people that were with me. They were in Santos and Sao Paolo. The children were shot by older street kids who were given a gun, a badge and a uniform.

GRUBER: Sorry to hear that.

COBHAM: Still to this day *(tearing up)* ... Excitement, oh man. I couldn't make it. I had to get out of that. I just said the magic words, I told the truth, I said what I saw, politically incorrect, that's all it took.

GRUBER: When did it happen? How did you find out? (We pause as the waiter serves our lunches.)

COBHAM: I found out about what happened within six months.

GRUBER: What significance does the title *Eggshells* have to those kids?

COBHAM: Boy smoked anything he could find on the street. He was very street wise. All he was missing was a mustache. They were put on the street because they were part of a family so big that there was no room in the house for the children. The smaller ones just were forgotten. Momma and poppa could not handle the rest. No food. They had to go out and find food and share and fend for themselves. Some went out and never came back. They found somebody else, they ran in packs. It took me to another level, frustration of not being able to help past teaching the kids, seeing them taking 1,000 cruzeiros which was 1/675,000th of a dollar to get something to eat.

GRUBER: How did you meet them? How old were they?

COBHAM: Happenstance. I ran into the boy who was allowed to keep a small swath of land to protect the cars on the street. I was with some UNICEF officials and we were walking by and the kid says, "1,000 cruzeiros and I promise nothing will happen to the car." They were 14. I didn't tell you about their kids.

Faina comes by to say hello. She is not happy with Bill's choice of lunch as I defend my spinach salad order. She promises to rejoin us later. I ask Bill what he means by "their kids."

COBHAM: Yeah, they had two kids. Welcome to the real world, Brian. They were trying to find food for their kids.

GRUBER: They were parents. At 14.

COBHAM: No momma and no poppa to speak of, they were on their own totally. Very bright. Lincoln and Paulette. Put a computer in front of him, an old Apple. He just pushed me out of the way, "Ooohh," only speaking in Portuguese.

GRUBER: How much time did you spend you with them?

COBHAM: I was there on three occasions. About six months off and on, trying to take part and make something happen.

GRUBER: That was a UNICEF project. Who else was involved?

COBHAM: No, no, just me. I had a band with Nico Assumcao, dead now, one of Brazil's greatest bass players. Pianist Luis Avelar, now living in Portugal. Trumpet player was Marcel Montarroyos, also passed away. Very fine musicians. We played concerts where these kids became our support. The heavy thing when I left, the last concert we played, Lincoln, I gave them each a U.S. one-dollar bill. And they became frightened. They knew what it was worth, 675,000 cruzeiros. But with the inflation rate rising out of control, the government changed the currency name from cruzeiros to cruzeiros real and lopped off three or four zeros. I remember there was a Grade A milk, a Grade B milk, Grade C, Grade D, Grade G milk. Less and less milk and more and more water or "filler." They had to figure out a way to buy that. He was not patient. When he spoke to me, I asked, "If you had your way, what would you like to accomplish in your life?" He said, "Learn English, have a business, take care of my family." There was a Chevrolet, a very cheap car by North American standards. He already knew, based on a normal salary in Brazil, it would take the rest of his life to get it. Gave him the dollar and their hands started shaking. They knew if they were seen with the dollar, they would be killed. Street kids were not supposed to have a dollar; to merchants and police, that meant that he had stolen it. He hid the dollar to figure out how to fence it off.

GRUBER: Tell me about their experience with music. Were you simply a father figure to them, were they interested in percussion?

COBHAM: No, Brazil has enough music, I learned from *them*. What I got from them, the pure reality of life. Back then there was a serious problem, one of the biggest natural bays in the world was Santos, a home to supertankers. A lot of these kids, in order to make money, would go out in makeshift boats; the girls would lure the sailors off and sleep with them on the boats, if they could not be smuggled on board the tankers. There was an AIDS epidemic no one wanted to acknowledge.

GRUBER: You were enjoying the kids event with the Soho school Tuesday. I must confess I cried as I watched. The interaction you were having with those kids, watching their faces. The first few songs were amazing. Some of them forgot their cues, some were really into it. When they sang that last song, *Billy Cobham*, man, the beatific look on your face. It was a beautiful moment. What were you feeling on that stage?

COBHAM: Can't put it into words. That's a very personal thing. Someone on the outside can give a word to it.

GRUBER: I'll help you with that (*laughter*).

COBHAM: That was a big surprise. When I first heard it at the school, oh man, I thought I was going to break down and cry. What, me?? I made this impression?

Now here's a heavy. Day before yesterday, I had a conversation with a black waitress (name withheld). I finished my spiel with the records (CD sales after the show) and all. She says, I have a question for you. "How do you do what you do?" I asked, "First, who are you and what do you do?" She said, "I'm a waitress here." "What else do you do?" "I write poetry, I am studying acting, working through the Ronnie Scott's Foundation. I am putting on a show." Then she paused and said, "I am planning to put on a show." Her hard face is starting to crack. She has dreams, the problem is, how to make those dreams reality? She asked, "How did you do it?" I said, "I was blessed. Not a lot of people can say that they want to be a writer, and do it. But you have to do it." She said, "I have all these things I want to put together." I said, "When it's right for you, then you do it." She said, "Yeah, but there must be some way." I said, "There is, be true to yourself. Do you really want to do this? Time's wasting. You're not going to be like this for the rest of your life." She starts to get meek as if I hit a (makes *buzzer* sound). "Get off your ass and if you really want to do this, block it out. Have a plan, lay out step a, b, c, d, accomplish these steps." She starts to cry. She says she is trying to understand, as a black man, you are not supposed to be able to do this. In her community, they fail, they drink. She has no one to look towards that is doing this stuff. She asked, "Can you write down something, can you give me some encouraging words?"

GRUBER: I think you just gave her a plan.

COBHAM: "I am going to give you three words. Just. Do. It. If you wait, you may die and never accomplish what you want."

GRUBER: I talked to Santiago before. I forgot that we met him and his dad Barry at your gig in Los Angeles. What is his role?

COBHAM: He has become an active member of the board of the Art of the Rhythm Section retreat. (A waiter comes by to clear the table.) He'd gone to WOMAD (World of Music Arts and Dance) as my proxy. He has spoken to Peter Gabriel's people. Barry and Peter Gabriel are very close friends. Santiago works for his dad from any place in the world. He came here on his own dime to help me because he believes in this.

GRUBER: I thought I heard backstage there is a possibility of recording this arrangement in studio.

COBHAM: Yes, not live, because of the intricacy of the parts. In Brazil, they did a six-month tribute to Miles. Once every two weeks they had a musician associated with Miles do a concert. I did the last one. I had to write my impression of what I thought was the one record that stood out for me and that was *E.S.P.* because that started the whole fusion era. That was THE band. Tony, Miles, Herbie, Wayne, and Ron.

GRUBER: What is the one most precious thing you learned from Miles?

COBHAM: To not be afraid of making mistakes. You know if you're gonna make one, make a big one. Make a move. Follow your gut.

GRUBER: Horace Silver?

COBHAM: Discipline, administration, learning how to say no. If you can't afford somebody, they gotta move on.

GRUBER: Billy Taylor?

COBHAM: Repertoire. I never had enough time to absorb what he could have told me. He was busy, doctor many times over, this was something very important to black people back then. Being associated with names that could get you to the next level. Playing with him, he never told me anything negative about my playing.

As we wrap our interview, TAMA executive Mike Shamada stops by to say hello. He's just arrived in London to see the final show. There is clearly a long-earned warmth and familiarity between the two. I ask Mike if he might be willing to share his perspective of his company's long-time association with Bill.

"Hoshino Gakki, owner of the Tama brand, entered into an artist endorsement with Billy Cobham in 1977," reminisces Shamada. "It was a sensational happening for Tama because the brand was born only three years before, while Billy's drumming style had a brilliant reputation in the drum community. Billy and Hoshino started to discuss new product ideas and once those ideas were realized and marketed, the reputation of Tama became solid." Shimada was instructed by the head office to mark their collaboration with a "big debut" at Frankfurt Messe, the world's largest trade fair, in 1978. "It was a big success. For Tama, Billy Cobham is an indispensable artist who brought the company vast success."

On my way to the club, Carl hails me on Old Compton Street to clarify one of his comments from our interview. Jazz puritans like Wynton Marsalis did many good things, he insists. They just had a fundamentalist view of their respective worlds. "When people like Wynton Marsalis come along with their dismissive attitude, I think, you've got to be kidding. That's my generation."

A Closing Night Conversation with Guy Barker

I make my way inside for a final backstage chat with bandleader Guy Barker.

GRUBER: It's closing night. How has the week gone for you? According to expectations?

BARKER: I think it has gone really well. I love the way that you can hear things develop. This week, come Wednesday, Thursday, it really sounded like a band. It was working, a lot. Last night one of the two tunes that causes the most amount of stamina-busting stuff actually felt like a walk in the park (*laughs*) so I felt, OK, we've got there. The thing is, the guys are really enjoying it a lot and you can see them smiling...

Guy orders a cappuccino, and the waiter asks about his dinner order. Drum cases lie in wait on the far end of the room for an efficient late-night departure.

BARKER: They admire Billy's work. They watch him and they are listening. There was one moment where he played this huge solo; it was actually an eight-bar break. He was doing one of his amazing things. All the guys were going, *we don't know where he is right now*, then suddenly Mike and Bill just went *BAM* right on the first beat of bar 9. It was perfect, stunning, and the whole band just started laughing. It's been a very happy, great experience. I have sensed that everybody is really looking forward to (closing night). Because when you do a run like this, the beginning of the week, you do your rehearsals, you do your sound check, then your daytimes you get on with what you have to do. Then it goes towards the rear end of the week, all that happens in the daytime is just a prequel to what's coming up, and time just disappears and suddenly you are back in the club and you are ready.

GRUBER: Even in the rehearsals, it was almost supernatural, the level of communication - trust was a term that you used - of comfortableness that everyone had. I was waiting for moments when there would be high anxiety or stress. That never happened.

BARKER: The most important thing is, first of all, just be nice. That's it. There are no prima donnas in the band. There are some people who, with the talent they have, you'd think they should be, but they aren't. The other thing is all the work that has gone in during the three months prior to this, with me locking myself away, and then checking absolutely every note on every part. Putting the scores into a friend of mine, Mark Cumberland, who is an amazing copyist, so that he creates the parts from my score that look beautiful on the page. That alone is half the battle.

GRUBER: Tell me how you did the opening for *Red Baron*, which is so much fun, just blows the audience away. Bill's friend David Shah said it starts like a '40s noir film, he expected Robert Mitchum to walk across the stage.

BARKER: I said to Bill we have to do *Red Baron* and I just sat down with a blank page - I didn't even use Bill's melody initially - and said I am not going to do that until I feel I am in the right place. And then as this introduction moves along, you start hearing hints of *Red Baron* so you know what's coming.

GRUBER: That's what Mike Hobart said, "I think I know where this is going."

BARKER: It's a way of saying, here is something for you from me. I hope you like this. You find a way to seamlessly get into the melody. It shows that it's a collaboration. I do that with *Obliquely* and *Eggshells*, it starts with my music, very much inspired by Bill's melodies, and then we land on Bill's melodies, chords and harmonies. It's just about being creative and being inspired by the situation.

GRUBER: Tell me the difference between Billy Cobham at Ronnie Scott's as bandleader of a quintet and Billy Cobham as the 17th member of a big band. How did you score against that and what was your experience watching him play that role?

BARKER: It's following Billy's routes, then taking a side street. What I am trying to get with the 17-piece is to have the orchestration definitely stated and adhered to, but with the feeling of freedom you get in a small group. We have got 17 guys and sometimes they are playing all at the same time, whereas in a small group you can state your theme and then off we go. And there is that freedom in it. And each night we can change the solo order around. This will be eight bars, this will be open. You get that complete freedom. I sent Bill copies of the scores so he can see what I had done. With his gig, he doesn't have any (sheet) music on the stage. He knows it. Now this is different. Bill is very carefully following the score but ultimately where he wants to be is without music. It's just two different ways of performing and we tried to meld them together.

GRUBER: What is Bill's place, to use Hobart's term, in the jazz or music firmament?

BARKER: Bill is unique inasmuch as he came out of a background with military stuff, he fell in love with jazz, playing straight-ahead jazz, then finding himself with Horace Silver's band. But then, suddenly, there he is in Dreams with Randy and Michael Brecker and a whole new thing is about to happen.

I remember as a kid, if my mum didn't know where I was on a Saturday, it was in a record shop. It was run by a guy called Al Merritt, a drummer, in

North Harrow, north London. I used to go in there at the age of 12, 13 and the guy was amazed, I would ask for records of Benny Goodman and Harry James. We struck up a friendship. I would go in there and he would play me stuff. He was into West Coast jazz. One day...when was Dreams?

GRUBER: '71 is Mahavishnu, so 69-71?

BARKER: Yeah, I went in there and he played me the very first Brecker Brothers album. I was 14/15, sitting with some friends. We had a little band and we had this idea, wouldn't it be great if you could have, like, a funky-soul rhythm section but mix it with bebop. We were talking about this and then I got a phone call. "Guy, *go to the record shop.*" Well, actually, I went in with Phil Todd, who is playing baritone (sax) in the show, and we went to the record store, and we put it on and we heard *Some Skunk Funk*, and then Michael Brecker's first break, and the two of us just went *mad*! This is unbelievable! This is like a whole new thing. At the time, I was obsessed with Clifford Brown and Freddie Hubbard and Miles. This is something so totally new, this sounds incredible. It came out of nowhere. There was a drummer called Phil James playing in the National Youth Jazz Orchestra with me and that is the first time I heard the name Billy Cobham. It must have been *Spectrum*, the first time. I never heard anything quite like it. And it kind of frightened me. I found it quite scary (*laughter*). I had to listen to it several times. It was the power of his playing. It kind of shocked me. Then I started checking some of the other stuff out, *Funky Thide of Sings*. Bill was the first drummer that people used that fusion term, jazz-rock, he was the first giant of that.

GRUBER: You shared with me how you met Bill. How did the big band project get started?

BARKER: We had worked with the hr Bigband in Frankfurt. Bill said, I would like you to do some more arrangements for me. It's always been a conversation. We had spoken about it many times. Use this, use that. Then this year, Bill said I got some new stuff and he set up this gig at Ronnie's and I said, yeah, I know exactly the right guys for it. And he sent me some new material and we wrote down a list together at my flat. Most of the things on that list are here. There's a couple that we didn't do.

I said to him, look Bill, you have reached a certain point in your life, you're a legend. And if I was going to do something for you, I would really like it to reflect your whole career. Bill said, what do you want to do? I said, well, how about *Light at the End of the Tunnel?* Great, yeah, let's do that. And I wrote down on a piece of paper, I found it the other day, in the corner I had written *BC Symphony*. And I had the idea of taking four or five of his tunes and making a complete piece out of them, each one of them linked together by one of my things. In the end, I made it the *BC Medley Part 1 and Part 2* so we cover *Stratus* and *Crosswinds* and all of that. I was looking at all these things, *Sal Si Puedes,* which is a real ballbuster. I just felt there was something else it needed and it was something to do with the balance of the sound.

Bill enters the room. I ask him if he got any rest. "Power nap!" he declares.

BARKER: I just went on to the computer and YouTubed this and Spotified that, everything. And then I came across this thing, *For All the Woman* and *Le Lis* and then I heard the original version and he said, don't do those. The version you want to base it on is the *Spectrum 40* one we did live. He sent that over. And then I just had fun with it. As soon as I heard that beautiful simple melody, four alto flutes, got to play that. To me that is what held the program together and gave it all the right things.

GRUBER: I saw a couple of YouTube videos about Brass for Africa. Is that a significant project for you?

BARKER: Brass for Africa is an amazing charity set up to help orphans in the slums of Kampala, Uganda. I met the guy, Jim Trott, a pilot for British Airways, at an event in Chile. He told me about this charity he was developing, teaching kids in this huge slum. I have become a patron.

There was a gang, 13/14-year-old kids terrorizing people. When the band was playing, they used to go in and the kids would get terrified and the priests would chase them away. One day, the gang came in and sat down and one of them came forth and said, please don't chase us away, we just want to hear the music. The priest said, if you guys stop this terrible behavior, stop being a gang, would you like to play in the band with us? If you are really good and don't do this anymore, I will see if I can get more instruments. On YouTube, there is a clip of this trombone player called Ronald who now teaches.

I spent a week out there. I cried and laughed every day. You couldn't believe the stories, these kids, their parents died of AIDS, they've been tortured. There was this one little kid, they said he hadn't spoken for three years. He was tortured. The day before, I was taking pictures of them on my camera. As I walked in the next day, there was this little guy, and he whispered in my ear, "Take a photo of me." They said, "He started speaking today." There is a girl called Lillian, who lost everything and took off with her brother and managed to get into Kampala.

When the Brass for Africa orphanage had been set up, this guy taught all these kids American Souza marches. He said, once you can play them by heart, we will march around the neighborhood. They were marching, playing and everybody is following. Lillian and her brother sat there and then they just joined in. The guy said, what's your name. Lillian. She told her story. He said, "Well, you're coming with us." Took her to the orphanage, to the dorm, said, "There is your bed, here's some food." And then they went and got a trumpet and put it on her lap and asked, would you like to play that. She said yeah. And that changed her life. And she came over here and did a concert. Ronald was the leader of that gang and now he is the sweetest guy in the world and he just got a degree in law. I introduced Jim to Alison Balsom, the great classical trumpet player and we both went to Kampala and Alison played a concert with Lillian. I did a concert with Alison at the Royal Albert Hall a few weeks ago and Ronald played as well.

Peak Experiences and What's Left Undone

As Bill prepares for the final night of the run, I present a hypothetical. "Let's say tonight after a good glass or two of wine, you fall asleep, and you have a dream about musicians, living or dead, that you'd love to play with. Any idea who those musicians would be?"

COBHAM: Yeah. I could see after all these years leaning toward singers more. Love to hear great vocalists present their ideas. I wouldn't mind working with Carmen MacRae, who I heard was a difficult person to work with, in terms of jazz. I would love to be in a band working with Joni Mitchell, I would love to work more with (Peter) Gabriel. The groove, especially with Tony Levin working with me, could be some very interesting stuff. After that, I could work with George (Benson), but the days of making solid LPs just for the instrumental aspect are far gone. A quartet with George, Herbie and Ron and myself? The last time I worked with Herbie Hancock was 2007, the birthday of Ron Carter at Carnegie Hall. Ron had three bands on the bandstand.

Bill lists the personnel playing the three combinations and said Carnegie Hall's stiff overtime policies and costs did not allow time for a closing performance of Bill, Wayne Shorter, Ron Carter, and Herbie Hancock. "Sounds like a good band right there," I joked, to which Bill answered, "Not bad, it's not a band that I would want to see any band follow." Jean-Luc Ponty was playing downstairs that night.

GRUBER: Have you played with Ponty?

COBHAM: Did I? (*Remembering*) I was in India, on the same stage. And I did a TV show, *Downbeat* Jazz Awards, in Chicago.

GRUBER: Who do you miss?

COBHAM: Wes Montgomery, a lot. Roland Hanna, great piano player, musician's musician. I would have loved to have had more years listening to a healthy Sarah Vaughan. Loved to have heard a healthy Bill Evans. Oscar Peterson. I would have loved to have been in the Basie band with Basie.

When I ask Bill if, looking back, there are peak experiences that are favorite memories, he answers, "Quite honestly, not." And then proceeds to riff on decades of shocking good stories and new characters.

COBHAM: I remember doing the jazz mass with the great Eddie Bonnamere,1966-67, when jazz masters were in abundance. I think he was Episcopalian; we were in St. Peter's Lutheran Church on 54th Street and Lexington Avenue. I was doing the Jazzmobile scene with Dr. Billy Taylor. I learned so much about the music. On Sundays, Reverend John Gensel, a great supporter, called 'the jazz pastor,' lectured on jazz, tying religion and jazz. He buried Dizzy Gillespie, and many others. I studied a lot, just brushing elbows with these people, they had a great view of things, and it affected me.

GRUBER: Any other interesting curious moments, unique influences? That's a great little story you shared.

COBHAM: One day led to the other. If you can imagine getting a call out of the blue – it happened quite often – from David Baker, a highly respected recording engineer. "Billy, you home, what are you doing?" In those days, I was doing *Promises, Promises*, Broadway pit shows. I wasn't working much, I had stopped working with Horace. I think I was separated from my first wife, I was on my own. He said, "Hey, why don't you come on over. There are some guys who are coming over to play." I never turned down a session. I go over to, what is it, Greenwich Park, in the middle of the village?

GRUBER: Washington Square Park?

COBHAM: That's it. He owned a brownstone right there. So, I walked in and I turn around, there is Chick Corea. It was like a railroad apartment; you just go from one room to the next. I come around the corner and there is Miroslav Vitous in the kitchen with an upright bass. In the bathroom is Wayne Shorter playing on the saxophone, whistling a melody. I'm going, *get outta here*, what's going on? He knew I had this unique drum set; there was a small shop called Professional Percussion Center run by a great cat Frank Ippolito. Al Duffy was the resident technician, he could build drums from scratch and was later contracted by Pearl to design their professional line. One day I told Al I could not have a whole set of drums, it was not only too expensive, it was too heavy for me to take to work on the existing surface bus line. Because at the time, there was no New York City bus line, there was the Bronx surface line, all different color buses, Green Line, Fifth Avenue Bus Line, Jamaica Bus Line, etcetera. I could get on the bus for 15 or 20 cents, if I played my cards right. I had a bass drum, and a floor tom, a rack-tom that could fit into it, so I could have my drums in one bass case, and my trap case with snare drum, stands, seat and cymbals in it. I could get on the back of the bus, walk to the front, pay the bus driver, go crosstown. I was young enough to carry it up the stairs without any problem, set up, sit down and wait to see who showed up. Out of the woodwork would come McLaughlin, Larry Coryell, Miroslav, Wayne, Joe Zawinul. From one day to the other we would just sit down and play things, just testing, see what was there. Mostly people I knew from a Miles session. "Hey, I got this thing I wanna try," from 10 in the morning to 5 in the afternoon. I can't recall even drinking a glass of water, there was so much going on. The payment was a quarter-inch tape of everything we did that day. Still have it but don't touch it because it would probably separate from the plastic backing.

GRUBER: Fantastic. Love it.

COBHAM: We just did things. If you ever get a chance to pick up, *Purple*, Miroslav Vitous. When Sony took over CBS, it went into CBS Legacy, a collector's item. When that record came out, it was after Miroslav had left Weather Report as its original bass player; by then Alphonso had come and left then Jaco was there. He put that record out and Joe never spoke to Miroslav again. Because he never asked permission. Pretty hip stuff despite the negative lingering aspect.

GRUBER: That was all recorded at that brownstone?

COBHAM: Absolutely. Miroslav held on to it until, finally, he needed some money, so, *boom*. The reason why I know is, I was working by then with my band. We go back to 1970 when we did this, and it never came out until 1975-76.

GRUBER: And you didn't get paid for that?

COBHAM: No, I didn't even know that we were supposed to.

GRUBER: Of course, at the time you didn't, you were a young man with a good heart having a great experience. Certain people would say, there is no copyright…

COBHAM: Not about this. To me, this is the closest I would ever come to being at the Colombe D'Or restaurant, south of France, fly on the wall, watching Picasso and friends sharing ideas. You don't get paid money for that! You have been paid just by being there at the right time. It was a monster, man. It just happened. Put something on. Play it. This came out years later. This is an, 'oh, by the way.' No one even thought about it. When Joe heard it, he got upset, he never got permission. Me? I was shocked. David Baker came to me, I met him in Atlanta, we were playing the Fox Theatre, he said, "Hey, man, I got some money for you." Gave it to me in one of his socks, like 500 bucks and change (*laughter*) and I'm going, "What is this?" He said, "This is the payment for the session you did."

GRUBER: Are there favorite houses for you to play?

COBHAM: No. Could easily say Ronnie's, it's my 10th or 11th year there. A club is a club. The ultimate is to be able to have a good solid monitoring system where I can hear all the material in perspective. When I get into my musical sound warp, it doesn't matter where I am.

GRUBER: In listening to *Spectrum* and reading about the history of Mahavishnu, Jan and Jerry expressed an interest in doing their own music both with and outside the band. You made that happen. Was that viewed by John as competitive or a distraction?

COBHAM: I don't know because he never spoke to me about it. This happened with my father as well. My father didn't view me as being anything to talk about. And despised me for my successes. Many people are treated this way by families. They have two routes to take. They can go down on themselves, be negative in life, striking out at the world and ending up losing. I started to do master classes. One of the classes was in Albuquerque, the city where he was living. I felt so blessed to be speaking to a full house of several thousand people about how I do what I do. The only person in the audience that was sitting there with a scowl on his face was my father.

That was 1978. But on the other side, what it reflects is, my positive direction through life has become a silent tool in defense of my persona. There are a whole lot of people in my family and outside who continue to compete with me on that level. Coming back to McLaughlin, my view is that he did not expect this. He was the golden child, the guy who was going to fill the vacuum that Jimi Hendrix left. And to some degree, for a short time, he did.

We are all responsible for the path that we take in life. I tend to not speak but *do*. The reason why I did not contribute to Mahavishnu was because I did not know how to write. I felt I should learn. The ideas that I had were not two-dimensional dots and lines on paper; I had to understand a lot of other things first and I am still doing that. So here I am.

GRUBER: You describe your dad as a boy in very affectionate terms.

COBHAM: I had a wall with that guy. He was already not living with us in '58-'59; he left my mom, me and my brother just before we left to go to New Brunswick on the other side of Brooklyn. Near what is now the Jackie Robinson Parkway but was the Interboro (the parkway connects Brooklyn and Queens, terminating at Jamaica Avenue in the Brooklyn neighborhood of East New York). I saw my dad with somebody else, a girlfriend or something, and I mentioned it to my mom because I thought it might be a friend of the family and she just blew a fuse. She knew a lot more than I knew and that's how it ended. I think I got beaten that night. Yeah. In West Indian families, children always got beat. Children always bore the burden of the frustrations of the parents. And there were some frustrations. The family didn't earn a lot of money. We found many ways to survive but in the end, mom and dad were very frustrated. We had to be careful what we said, how we dressed. I couldn't learn Spanish, why, because I was in America. The language didn't matter because the music had so much more strength and weight. I didn't give a shit if it was English or Irish. The music was first and foremost, because it felt good and it was truer than any words that could be said anyway. In the process, my father was trying to make points, intellectual points, because he was a very clever guy. Mathematics was a gift to him. He had a great mind. He was very creative in terms of the musical thing but one of the things he missed was he wanted to control every note everyone was playing. That's where he lost. He only started to write music after he saw I was successful writing music.

I made 50 different projects under my name and my recording company, 20 records. This comes out of a need to survive in a good way. Hungry. Where musicians are comfortable and have achieved a certain level, they don't want to go anywhere else because they found this point where people are cheering, "Yay, 'XYZ!' Yeah!" They play to a large number of listeners, now they have arrived. Only one band I can recall I felt close to intimately, never felt that way, and that was Weather Report. Unfortunately, they didn't stay together because they had other issues. One being, I'm sure, ego. Who is better than whom, which is another sick part of the music business. That's the musician's fault for not being able to identify or relate or show respect for their colleagues in a way to allow the whole band to stay together as a cohesive unit and project their personalities. All of these are elements that make for a special artist. One that not only plays by themselves but who can play with everybody else and be comfortable doing it. I'm always happy to play anybody's music. In the pecking order of musicians, who is higher than whom, drummers are far down the pike. They are generally not considered musicians. They are supposed to support the other musicians.

GRUBER: How old were you when you went out with your dad to gigs?

COBHAM: I think I was six or seven.

GRUBER: Did that happen often?

COBHAM: I don't remember doing it more than once or twice. On one side, it's bright and on the other side it's dark. I can remember going to a Brooklyn Dodgers versus New York Giants game at the Polo Grounds with my dad once. I can remember going to Empire Boulevard to Ebbets Field. I can remember my dad buying a bicycle for me which was promptly stolen in two days by bigger kids in Bed-Stuy, which was a very tough neighborhood. And my dad coming home to try and find that bicycle. After that, everything that happened with me and my father was confrontational. My mom was not often upset with me, but when she was, she told my dad and I knew I was going to get a spanking, beaten.

GRUBER: Was there a time when he observed you getting interested in music, took pride, engaged with you?

COBHAM: He brought me to a club. I played the drums and he played with me. After I was a professional musician, he would sit in. His problem was he was too much of a singular player, he played for himself while onstage with other musicians. That's a big difference. I used to play a lot of dances in my early twenties before I went into the army, 1962-1964. I went in the army at the end of '64. I came out in '68. I played in the Bronx, near Yankee Stadium and the 168th Street Armory where they had shows, with catering. My dad sometimes showed up. Later on, he had a concert and I remember Ron Carter, Hubert Laws, and Jimmy Owens played with my dad. That was the last time I remember working with him. Those guys were amazingly gracious.

GRUBER: How did your mom respond to your success in music?

COBHAM: My Mom? Always there. During the first Gulf War, my mom was supporting me in Rome, cooking, making sure my clothes were clean. I was working everyday on a project. She was my main ally. I brought her to have someone to talk to.

GRUBER: When did they pass?

COBHAM: My mom, 2006. My dad, 2005.

GRUBER: They both, especially your dad, must have been very proud to see the level of prominence you achieved.

COBHAM: I think he did. But here's the kicker. He was not a great dad. That comes from our upbringing, what filters down from one generation to the next. In Panama, we were a poor family. The whole psychology was to keep a sense of family. My mom was alone. My father was pitted as the threat; if we didn't do anything that was right even though he wasn't there, he was the heavy. Even on the phone, we were so intimidated by him, we had to be careful because I don't want to get hurt, to get hit. There was always the fear of pain being inflicted on us. Even seeing him was painful, even in the days leading to his death. It wasn't a very positive thing. The only way I could deal with it was to be as positive to him as I possibly could. The only thing I could not do was to give him acknowledgment for his support of me throughout my career because of what he did to me and my family. Not just by not being there, but we were second class in his eyes. It wasn't because he wanted to be. I think that he was looking for something more. He was a very intelligent man, but he was weak in other ways. He wasn't strong enough to see the value of family, to respect his wife and his two sons.

Every record I made, I paid tribute to my mom, my then-wife, my daughters, people who were really close to me. But I never mentioned his name. Thirty records later, when he was in a senior citizens environment, he is talking me up for all the things I had done, because he is competing with the other guys who had families and were preaching the positive aspects of their people. It finally comes back around. A guy sees my records in my father's collection and he says, one thing I can't figure out, how come your name is never mentioned in the records? It broke my father down. He spoke to my mother. When I saw him, I said, you understand why, right? He could not say yes or no.

GRUBER: I was watching the *Sonic Mirror* DVD. At the end, there was a credit to your dad.

COBHAM: The musicians included Yoruba relatives of mine from Nigeria. My father played, *For All We Know We Will Never Meet Again*. That was the last time I saw him alive. He died six months later.

It's time to wrap up our afternoon conversation so that Bill can prepare for closing night, I ask if he has a model at this point in life, an outlook.

COBHAM: Benny Golson: live life in moderation. Manage your time. Don't do anything more than you need to do. Relaxed, laid back. Control the stress in your life. Some people in my life are really special. Peter Gabriel is one. Another is Santiago Roberts. I'm a fan of Phil Collins.

GRUBER: Why?

COBHAM: Sincerity, simplicity. Phil played who he was. Walked the walk, doing what he felt, from the heart. When you can do that, you have arrived. When you have a marketing apparatus behind you that can promote that, then you really have arrived.

GRUBER: There was a time when you were voted best drummer in the world year after year. Did that ever matter to you?

COBHAM: No. Of course, it made me feel good that somebody noticed what I was sharing with the world. But the next day, I still had to have enough money to get on the bus. Some people are gullible enough to need that to spur them on. There is music to be played and created and that is more important to me than receiving acknowledgement of what I have already accomplished in the guise of a plastic loving cup.

GRUBER: Why do you continue to create?

COBHAM: I feel like James Michener. You know how many books he wrote? For me, I am playing my life. Every time I write, it's based on something that I've been through or experienced, something that inspired me. I wrote this tune called *Red Moon*. Last year we had a red moon. It inspired me to write this piece that we are rehearsing now to be on the next record. If you go back to *Crosswinds*, I was sitting in Hiroshima next to a shadow that used to be a person when the bomb went off. It inspired me to write *Heather*. When I then see it used as the background music in the video presenting the tsunami that was created in Sendai, it's dramatic. And that's what music is all about, Brian. For, me, it's my life.

GRUBER: Anything left undone in your career?

COBHAM: I never thought about it. This is what I do. Playing music is what keeps me alive.

During the final show, as Mark Phinney luxuriates in a Buffalo Trace old-fashioned mixed by Ronnie Scott's top shelf bartender Andre, he declares the band is "grooving flawlessly," the songs increasing in emotional power. We are transfixed, giddy at the final climax of the final performance. A young man and woman chat and laugh loudly as the prelude to *Red Baron* thrills the audience. Twice I turn to them to say something, then remember I saw them with band members and should probably leave it alone. I saw Bill and his band perform at the open-air Rio das Ostras Jazz and Blues Festival in Brazil and was standing in the crowd as a small group of guys talked loudly in Portuguese. Under a stormy Saturday night sky, they just wouldn't shut up, so I intervened, and told them in English to *please be quiet*. They were stunned; I made sure I eyed a secure exit when the show was over.

At what point is a finale not mere entertainment but the completion of a heroic journey? The week began with certain challenges, with *Sal Si Puedes* at one end and *Red Baron* at the other. Each night, each musician took hold of the music, each night it was noticeably better. Most of the guys saw the music last week for the first time. This final performance now takes on the feeling of a celebration. They did it. They won. They have slain their dragons.

I turn to the couple behind me at the bar and instruct them, *this is a sacred moment*, so, please stop talking. They do and the finale is spectacular. Three horn players trade riffs, building to a rip-roaring finish.

A little past midnight, as is the club's business practice, a smaller band takes the stage to entertain into the wee hours. Band members circulate, gleeful, backslapping and reminiscing about fine moments, proud of the week's work. One of the trumpeters approaches me with a smile, "Have enough material?" Most of these guys worked for well under their usual scale, in tribute to Bill, but even more so because they simply "never say no to Guy."

As I talk to two band members, I feel a strong, sudden grasp of my left upper arm. Guy Barker, slightly disheveled and enjoying his post-show experience immensely, demands in a firm tone, "Do not leave the club until you hear my last joke."

Later, backstage, Bill and Faina, friends David and Hildegard Shah, Guy and I enjoy a final rest before clearing out. At precisely the right moment, after a dramatic pause, Guy launches into his final joke of the week. A few meters away, Ronnie Scott himself regaled audiences with his stand-up humor. Guy tells me he used to stop in to the office to say hello and Ronnie would look up and ask if he had any jokes.

Guy makes me promise not to repeat the joke (I think he was kidding), though I tried out alternate versions on a few friends and could not get the punchline right. Suffice it to say it's about a difficult marriage, a pub, and a lot of snails. I am enthralled, and comforted that the week ends as it started, with Bill's full-throated laugh. The same laugh that launched the *Spectrum* album in the first five seconds of *Quadrant Four*.

As everyone begins clearing out, it is getting on to 2am, I find myself alone in the backstage lounge. I survey the space one last time, the now-full drum cases, the left-behind paraphernalia, the personal effects waiting to be gathered. Then I notice something that seems familiar. It is a hand-crafted gift from the Soho school kids, containing the lyrics of the song they wrote for him. Cut-out letters on top saying, "Thank you, Billy," with hand-written lyrics on a purple sheet pasted on a light background. By now, most of them will have forgotten about much of the experience, a pleasant field trip with that nice jazz guy. Many will cherish it as a special memory. And one or two might be awake this very moment, staring at the ceiling and reliving the scene, determined to make their own mark one day soon. *To light up the sky and make people fly.*

He's a time keeper, the heartbeat of the band.
Fast as lightning, you can barely see his hands.
He's as loud as thunder, then as soft as snow.
Don't you know, he's always in the groove. Billy Cobham is in the groove.

He's from Panama with a New York City move.
He'll make your band go far when he's playing in the groove.
When he plays, the gates of Heaven open wide,
Every day making music here inside.
Time divider see your name on lights,
Groove inspirer set us free.

He can shake the time,
Make this music mine.
Keep us all in line,
Watch us shine.

Billy Cobham - he's a legend, an inspiration.
Billy Cobham, lights up the sky.

Billy Cobham - he's a music sensation,
Billy Cobham, you make us fly (so high).

ABOUT THE AUTHOR

Brian Gruber has been creating, innovating, and marketing new forms of media for forty years. Born in Brooklyn, New York, he earned a B.A. from Queens College, City University of New York in Communication Arts and Sciences, and an M.A. from Pepperdine University in broadcast journalism and management.

Gruber was the first head of marketing for the *C-SPAN* public affairs network, where he hosted two weekly live call-in shows with politically prominent guests such as Cesar Chavez, Nancy Pelosi, and John McCain. He was the first head of marketing for *FOXTEL*, Australia's leading national cable television system. Gruber was founder and CEO of *FORA.tv*, which brought premiere public forums to the web, selected by *Time* magazine as one of the 50 best sites on the web. While at FORA, Gruber continued his fascination with long-form televised conversations, interviewing scores of guests from Christopher Hitchens, Norman Mailer, and Malcolm Gladwell to Jim Lehrer, Louis Rossetto, and Quincy Jones. He founded *ShowGo.tv*, an automated video platform streaming hundreds of live jazz concerts from elite clubs around the world, adding, of course, backstage conversations with performers.

Gruber has served as media consultant to several dozen global clients from San Francisco's World Affairs Council to the European Journalism Centre. He is the author of one novel, *Dauphin, Dorian and Dead* and the Kickstarter-funded political travelogue *WAR: The Afterparty*, interviewing soldiers, jihadis, revolutionaries, mothers, journalists, ex-presidents, and eyewitnesses while exploring the human and financial costs of a half century of U.S. military interventions from both sides of the gun barrel. After landing in Cambodia at the conclusion of that round-the-word journey, Gruber relocated to Koh Phangan, Thailand, to write by the sea and help others share their stories.

BILLY COBHAM DISCOGRAPHY

Each book chapter has a Spotify playlist (Billy Cobham One, Billy Cobham Two, etc.) including relevant tunes, artists, and genres. Enjoy each chapter's soundtrack.

1970s

Billy Cobham - Spectrum (Atlantic Records) - 1973

Billy Cobham - Crosswinds (WEA)

Billy Cobham - Total Eclipse (WEA)

Billy Cobham - Shabazz (WEA)

Billy Cobham - A Funky Thide Of Sings (WEA)

Billy Cobham - Life and Times (WEA)

Billy Cobham - Cobham/Duke Live (WEA)

Billy Cobham - Magic (WEA)

Billy Cobham - Inner Conflicts (WEA)

Billy Cobham - Simplicity of Expression - Depth of Thought

Billy Cobham - B.C. (rare)

Billy Cobham - Anthology (Rhinophonic)

1980s

Billy Cobham - Flight Time (InAkustik)

Billy Cobham - Stratus (InAkustik)

Billy Cobham - Observations & Reflections (Elektra/Musician)

Billy Cobham - Smokin' (Elektra/Musician)

Billy Cobham - Warning (GRP Records) - 1985

Billy Cobham - Power Play (Eagle Records) - 1986

Billy Cobham - Picture This (Eagle Records) - 1987

Billy Cobham - Incoming (K-tel)

1990s

Billy Cobham - By Design (Finac) - 1992

Billy Cobham - The Traveler (101 South Records) - 1994

Billy Cobham - Nordic (Rhythmatix Records) - 1996

Billy Cobham - Nordic / Off Color (Eagle Rock)

Billy Cobham - Focused (Eagle Records) - 1998

Billy Cobham - Mississippi Nights Live (Wenlock)

Billy Cobham - Ensemble New Hope Street (Eagle Records) - 1999

Billy Cobham - North by NorthWest (Creative MultiMedia Concepts)

Billy Cobham - Paradox - Paradox (Enja)

Billy Cobham - Paradox - First/Second (Enja)

Billy Cobham - Best Of (Atlantic)

2000 - today

Billy Cobham - Live in Rome (Audio Records) - 2000

Billy Cobham - Art of Three (In and Out Records) - 2001

Billy Cobham - Culture Mix (In and Out Records) - 2002

Billy Cobham - Culture Mix - Colours (In and Out Records) - 2004

Billy Cobham - The Art of Four (In and Out Records)

Billy Cobham - North by Northwest (Nicolosi Productions) - 2005

Billy Cobham - Drum and Voice (Nicolosi Productions) - 2005

Billy Cobham - Meeting of the Spirits (In and Out Records) - 2006

Billy Cobham - Drum 'n' Voice Vol. 2 (Nicolosi Productions) 2006

Billy Cobham - The Art of Five (In and Out Records)

Billy Cobham - Fruit from the Loom (CMMC Records) - 2007

Billy Cobham - Drum 'n' Voice Vol. 3 (Nicolosi Productions) - 2010

Billy Cobham - Palindrome (BHM Productions) - 2010

Billy Cobham - Live in Leverkusen (BHM Productions GmbH) - 2011

Billy Cobham - Compass Point (Purple Pyramid) – 2013

Billy Cobham - Tales from the Skeleton Coast – 2014

Billy Cobham - Spectrum 40 Live - 2015

Billy Cobham - Drum 'n' Voice Vol. 4 (Nicolosi Productions) – 2016

Billy Cobham & Frankfurt Radio (hr) Big Band – Broad Horizon - 2016

Printed in Great Britain
by Amazon